跨文化视角下的北美与中国文化

Kuawenhua Shijiaoxia de Beimei yu Zhongguo Wenhua

[加] 李盈 王健 著

CROSS-CULTURAL PERSPECTIVES: NORTH AMERICA AND CHINA

Yvonne Li Walls and Jan W. Walls

图书在版编目（CIP）数据

跨文化视角下的北美与中国文化／（加）李盈，（加）王健著．－－北京：高等教育出版社，2014.5
ISBN 978-7-04-038142-9

Ⅰ．①跨… Ⅱ．①李… ②王… Ⅲ．①比较文化-研究-北美洲、中国 Ⅳ．①G04

中国版本图书馆CIP数据核字（2014）第058671号

策划编辑	刘清田	责任编辑	孙海芳	封面设计	张志奇	版式设计	王艳红
责任校对	陈 杨	责任印制	毛斯璐				

出版发行	高等教育出版社	网　址	http://www.hep.edu.cn
社　址	北京市西城区德外大街4号		http://www.hep.com.cn
邮政编码	100120	网上订购	http://www.landraco.com
印　刷	北京鑫丰华彩印有限公司		http://www.landraco.com.cn
开　本	787mm×960mm 1/16		
印　张	8.25		
字　数	120千字	版　次	2014年5月第1版
购书热线	010-58581118	印　次	2014年5月第1次印刷
咨询电话	400-810-0598	定　价	48.00元

本书如有缺页、倒页、脱页等质量问题，请到所购图书销售部门联系调换
版权所有　侵权必究
物　料　号　38142-00

作 者 简 介

李盈（Yvonne Li Walls）：美国华盛顿大学硕士，印第安纳大学准博士，主修比较文学。曾任教于美国华盛顿大学、印第安纳大学、明尼苏达大学、台湾师范大学、台湾大学、日本爱知大学、加拿大比西大学、维多利亚大学和西门菲莎大学等。曾出版英译中和中译英之作品多项。

王健（Jan W. Walls）：美国印第安纳大学硕士及博士，主修中国语文。曾任教于美国印第安纳大学、日本爱知大学、加拿大比西大学、维多利亚大学和西门菲莎大学等。曾出版英译中国诗歌及文章多篇。

李盈与王健合作之主要出版物包括：英译郑板桥和王闿运诗多首，制罐巷（Cannery Row 之中译本），100 Allegorical Tales From Traditional China（《寓言故事百则》之英译本），West Lake: A Collection of Folktales（《西湖民间故事》之英译本），英译《中国名家绘画》（60卷），Classical Chinese Myths 与 Using Chinese。

序

　　我们两人在北美几所大学将近四十年教中国语言和进行跨文化交流的过程中，北美的学生时常问："为什么要这样说？"或"为什么这样做？"其实我们本来可以很简单地就回答说："因为十三亿的中国人认为这样才合理。"但是，我们总是很详细地给他们解释英文与中文不同的说法和思考方式终归是以不同的形式来观察和表现同样的现象。不同的文化价值观和表现方式也是同样的道理。我们在这本书里也多次提醒读者，北美和中国文化中的许多表面上的差异终究是"殊途同归"的。

　　由于世界观的不同，所以每个人都可能从很多不同的角度去预测、观察、描写或解释任何社会情景。比如，美国人或加拿大人去中国朋友家做客的时候带了一盒巧克力作为礼物。中国朋友将巧克力收下，然后就收起来。美国人或加拿大人就会觉得中国朋友不喜欢这份礼物，所以就藏起来了。要不然为什么不打开与大家共享呢？相反，如果中国人去北美朋友家做客，带一盒巧克力作为礼物。他的北美朋友将其打开，拿出来与大家共享时，他倒会愣一下。北美人也许不知道中国朋友不会当着别人的面打开他们的礼物以示客气，以免与别人的礼物比较，或使客人不好意思。而中国人也许不知道，在北美，主人要把礼物打开、与别人共享以示感激之意。

　　这本书是用中文和英文两种语言写的。两种语言的内容都有同样的大题目和分题，但内容不尽相同。首先，我们比较了日常观念，如：地址、日期、时间、姓名和称呼的不同表现方式。从这些不同的表现方式，我们立刻可以看出来，虽然它们很不同，但是每一种方式都表达了其情况所需求的信息，所以绝对没有哪一种方式是对或哪一种方式是错的问题。其实，只是殊途同归而已。接着，我们比较了有如餐饮和座位、送礼、迎接和告别，以及感谢和道歉等日常之事的形成、组织和表达的文化逻辑。我们注意到并讨论北美和中国对于颜色、数字、动物和鸟类，以及花卉和植物的象征意义的相同和互异，以促进双方的互相了解。然后，我们讨论一些已经习以为常的体态语，如眼光的接触、触摸、互相协调、静默和手势等的差异，以增进互相的了解。

最后，我们做了一项非常有启发性的比较：比较北美英语里和中文里的谚语智慧，从而显示了两种文化以不同的说法表达了基本上相同或相似的传统智慧。这也许是最有力的、可以支持我们所要证实的"表面上的差异并非真正的差异"的论点：这两种文化是"殊途同归"的。

李盈、王健于加拿大温哥华

目 录

导言 ·· 1

社会交往 ·· 6

地址、日期和时间 ·· 6
名字和称呼 ·· 9
名片 ·· 10
个人、团体与家庭 ·· 10
人际关系 ·· 11
直爽与含蓄 ·· 12
进餐与座位 ·· 13
礼物 ·· 14
迎接与送别 ·· 15
对年龄的态度 ·· 16
感谢与道歉 ·· 17

II 跨文化视角下的北美与中国文化

象征意义 ································· 18
颜色 ································· 18
数字 ································· 21
动物与鸟类 ·························· 24
花卉与植物 ·························· 28

体态语与手势 ····························· 31
体态语 ······························· 31
体态与手势 ·························· 35
不礼貌的举止 ······················· 41

谚语的智慧 ································ 42

导　　言

西方有个说法：

天堂里：
- 警察是英国人
- 厨师是法国人
- 情人是意大利人
- 所有的事都是由德国人组织的

而地狱里：
- 警察是法国人
- 厨师是英国人
- 情人是德国人
- 所有的事都是由意大利人组织的

也有人指出，对东亚人来说：

最好的人生是因为拥有：
- 日本妻子
- 中国厨师
- 美国房子

最糟的人生是因为拥有：
- 中国房子
- 日本厨师
- 美国妻子

很多人都会觉得以上的说法很幽默，因为其看法过于简单并且一概而论。正面地看，这些说法指出了不同民族和不同文化里一些很明显的特点。但我们都得切记：不是所有的法国人都是好厨师，而且不是所有的意大利人都是好情人。当然日本妻子不都是顺服的妻子，中国房子按西方标准来说也不都是很挤而不理想的房子。

所以，这就产生了用不同文化做比较的机会，同时也就产生了拿不同文化来比较的陷阱。我们要切记，以比较的方式来研究文化的时候，只能选用文化中比较突出的特色。虽然这些特色不一定是所比较的民族里每个人都有的特色，然而，为了避免有人会说"那个国家的人都是一样的"，我们一定要努力去了解不同国家的人和文化。

不同的民族之间，都会有文化差异。然而，差异并不是差错。虽然差异是混乱的渊源，但差异也是能量的渊源，以及动力的来源。以水为例，要是没有水平的差异，水就不会流动，就会变成死水。只有差异才能使水流动。

著名的神话学家约瑟夫·肯伯（Joseph Campbell, 1904—1987）说得好：

"世界上明显的差异是次要的。虽然世界上有各种相反事物存在,但是,我们却都共同有一种虽为隐形的但经验过的一致性和同一性。"
(摘自 Joseph Campbell:《千面英雄》[The Hero with a Thousand Faces]. London: Fontana-Harper, 1993, 第162页。)

不同的文化之间当然有明显的差异,但是进行跨文化研究和要了解不同文化,我们就一定要记住:作为人类,我们在本质上是相似的。中国人自古就知道这个道理。过去每个受教育的人都要背诵的第一本书《三字经》的第一句就说:"人之初,性本善。性相近,习相远。"

图1　不同不是不对;差异不是差错　李盈作

如果我们能使每个人都一样,那么生活和人类的交往不是就会容易了解一点吗?但是既然我们不能也不应该使每个人和每种文化都变得一样,既然我们应该保持文化之间的差异,从而我们的世界才会更为多彩多姿并更美丽,我们就需要更进一步去了解不同的文化和文化差异的意义。通过比较的方式,我们就能更进一步地了解不同的人,并且更进一步减少文化之间的冲突和不同文化之间的误解。

4 跨文化视角下的北美与中国文化

比较加拿大、美国和中国的不同

表1 比较加拿大、美国和中国的不同

国家	加拿大	美国	中国
面积	9,984,670平方公里（世界第二大国，仅次于俄罗斯）	9,826,675平方公里（世界第三大国）	9,596,961平方公里（世界第四大国，次于俄罗斯、加拿大、美国）
人口	34,568,211（世界第三十七）	316,668,567（世界第三）	1,349,585,838（世界第一）
人口密度	每平方公里3.5人	每平方公里32人	每平方公里137人
邻国	美国	加拿大，墨西哥	阿富汗、不丹、缅甸、印度、哈萨克斯坦、朝鲜、吉尔吉斯斯坦、老挝、蒙古、尼泊尔、巴基斯坦、俄罗斯（东北）、俄罗斯（西北）、塔吉克斯坦、越南
民族	来自不列颠群岛28%；来自法国23%；来自其他欧洲国家15%；原住民2%；其他6%；混合背景26%	白人79.96%，黑人12.85%，亚洲人4.43%，原住民0.97%，其他	汉族91.5%；55个少数民族，8.5%
国语	英语58.8%，法语21.6%，等	英语（多数人）	普通话
城市人口	71%	82%	47%

鉴于以上的比较（见表1），我们可以看出：无论从地理、社会和文化等方面来说，中国比加拿大和美国复杂得多了，特别是人口多、邻国多。然而，加拿大有二百多个国家的移民，美国也有将近一百个国家来的移民，是移民国家；而中国不是个移民国家，移民非常少。

加拿大有一个邻国，五个半时区；美国有两个邻国，六个时区；而中国有十四个邻国，却只有一个时区。这至少可以表明：加拿大人和美国人在时间观方面比较复杂，而中国人在时间观方面比较集中化，也比较统一。这种复杂和统一，也会表现在其他方面。

跨文化交流研究的前提
- 相同点多于差异点
- 差异常被过于强调
- 文化是殊途同归的

跨文化交流研究的目的
了解不同文化，从而减少异文化之间的冲突和误解。

北美和中国文化的特点摘要

表2　北美和中国文化的特点摘要

北美	中国
注重独立	注重互相依存
视个人为重要	视个人为团体的一部分
视了解自己为最重要	人际和睦为最重要
视平等为重要	接受等级为必要的
视争论为达到真理的途径	视公开的交锋为分歧
视成功为个人的成就	将成功归功于团体的努力
视隐私为重要	不特别注重隐私

社会交往

地址、日期和时间

语言是交流的媒介，所以也表达文化。英文俗语说："照顾小钱，大钱自然来。"(Take care of the dimes and the dollars will take care of themselves.) 从一方面来说，在加拿大和美国等英语国家，在出发点、表达和行动等方面，总是由小到大。然而，中国人却说："大处着眼，小处着手。"这就表明中国人通常看重大处，却从小事着手去做。下面我们将通过具体例子和场景来比较北美和中国文化的特点。

地址

用英文在信封上写地址，以横写的方式，其次序如下：
- 收信人姓名
- 号码 + 街名
- 城市名 + 省名
- 国名

例： Mr. John Smith
　　　4444 Walnut Street
　　　Vancouver, B.C.
　　　Canada

用中文在信封上写地址，横着写则次序正好与英文相反：
- 国名
- 省名 + 城市名
- 街名 + 号码
- 收信人姓名

例：中国
　　　山东济南
　　　古亭街8888号
　　　吴慈仁（收）

日期

用英文表达日期时，其次序通常是：
- 星期几
- 日
- 月
- 年
- 某日

例：It was Friday, the 28th of December, 2012 that day.

用中文表达日期时，其次序为：
- 某日
- 年
- 月
- 日
- 星期几

例：那天是2012年12月28日，星期五。

时间

英文：

- 分
- 秒（过）
- 点钟

例：It is now 3 minutes and 20 seconds past 5 o'clock.

中文：

- 点钟
- 分
- 秒

例：现在是5点3分20秒。

从以上的例子中，我们可以看出几乎所有用英文述说地址、日期和时间的时候，是以个人或较小单位在顶上的金字塔形。相反，用中文述说地址、日期和时间的时候，是以个人或较小单位在底层的反金字塔形。这反映出在北美文化中个人是被视为比较重要的，而在中国文化中个人是被视为不太重要的。在中国文化中，个人总是属于一个较大的单位，如家庭、宗族或社会。

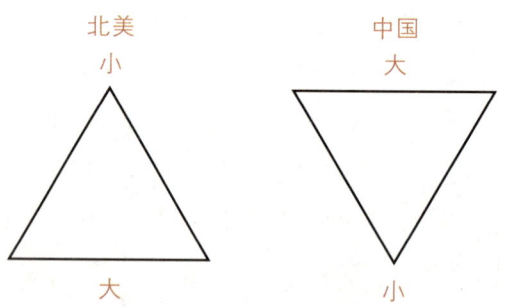

图2　北美和中国述说地址、日期和时间的比较　李盈作

名字和称呼

在北美，一个人的全名包括人名、中间名和姓，但有些人也许没有中间名。其次序是：名 + 中间名 + 姓，例如：Mary Allen Smith。除了在正式场合以外，一般人介绍或自我介绍的时候都多用名而不太用全名。通常介绍的时候用名不用姓也是一种表示友好和亲近的方式。一般，妇女结婚后就采用丈夫的姓而不用自己本来的姓，但也有保留自己的姓而把丈夫的姓加在最后的。比如说，Mary Allen Smith，她结婚后的全名可以是 Mary Allen Jones, Mary Allen Smith Jones 或 Mary Smith Jones，她就是 Jones 夫人或 Jones 太太。儿子的名字可以与父亲完全相同，只加一个"小"（Junior, Jr.）字即可。例如，John Barrie Jones 的儿子可以叫 John Barrie Jones, Jr.。然而，女儿的名字却不能用母亲的名字后面加"小"字。较正式地称呼人的时候，可以用：头衔+姓，如，President Jones, Dr. Smith, Professor Wilson 等。但一般的头衔，如主任、经理、老师、师傅等，在英文却不能用。那就用：Mr.（先生）、Mrs.（太太）、Ms.（女士）、Miss（小姐）等。

在中国，有些少数民族，如苗族、蒙古族与藏族，会采用复姓。就中国的汉人来说，全名包括姓和名，其次序为：姓 + 名。姓，一般是单姓，也有复姓的。名可以是单名或者双名。一般没有中间名。所以，汉人的名字最长的是四个字。

图3　中国的介绍方式："这位是王主任，这位是李经理。两位，这是我们的总裁，约翰！"　李盈作

如果名为两个字，则第一个字可能是代表辈分。那么，同一辈的儿子和男孩名字里都会有那个字。女孩名字也可以如此，但并不如男孩的普遍。由此可见，传统的观念是男孩比较重要，因为男孩可以传宗接代。但是，儿子的名字不能像西方一样与父亲的相同，因为那就太不尊敬了。现在，妇女结婚后，不必改名换姓。最尊敬的称呼人的方式是：姓+头衔，比如：李校长、王教授、刘主任、张老师、钱师傅等。有头衔的，称呼的时候，最好都用头衔。

名　　片

在北美，人们，特别是有事业的人或有身份的人，见面的时候都会交换名片。但是，交换的方式会比较随便。一方把名片递给对方而已；而且，通常只用一只手。

有相当一段时间，中国人一般不用名片。但改革开放以后，交换名片就很普遍了。近年来，凡是有事业的和有公务的人都会在第一次见面时交换名片。交换名片最好的方式是用双手将自己的名片递过去，也用双手将对方的名片接过来，以示敬意。最理想的方法是先仔细地把名片看一看才收起来，以表示对对方的重视。

个人、团体与家庭

在英文的书面用语中，"我（I）"字，当主词时，无论在句子什么部位总是大写的，而且虽然已是很明显的主词，在句子中都不能省略。但是"你（you）"和其他的代词却只有当主词的时候才大写。这显示出"我"（也叫"第一人称"）与"你"、"他"、"她"和"它"相对比是多么重要。"我"这个字在英文里的大写也象征着个人在北美社会中被视为最基本的元素。个人的"隐私"也是一种必须尊重的重要概念。"独立"的概念也是一样重要。有个人主义观的人也怕会和别人一样。比如说，人们通常会想要赶上式样和颜色的时髦。然而一个人自己的式样和颜色的组合却最好要与众不同，否则甚至会觉得有点丢脸。大人鼓励小孩子从小就独立：一旦小孩子能自己梳洗、吃饭和做别的事，大人就让小孩子自己做。独立是值得敬佩和模仿的。放假的时候，人们喜欢远离"使人发狂的群众"，到清静的地方去独处。正是由于这种个人和独立观念的重要性，北美社会也比较平等，这也可以说明为什么北美的权威人物常会被批评和讽刺到一般旁观的中国人会大为吃惊的程度。这是因为普通大众是通过选举把政权托付给有权力的政治人物的。在加拿大和美国，我们常会看到许多卡通、幽默说笑家，以及喜剧讽刺和嘲笑政治家和权威人物。

然而，在中文里的"我"字，无论是主词还是受词，总是不变的。并且，无论在书面用语或对话中，主题一明显就可以省略掉"我"字，不必时时重复。如果时时重复，反而给人一种自大的感觉。很多世纪以来，"隐私"这个观念对大多数人是不存在的。近年来，这个观念开始对有些人有些重要性了。可是，用中文的"隐私"翻译英文的"privacy"失去了英文里的一些好意，而加上了一些英文里没有的反面意思。在中国文化里，互相依存比独立向来都重要得多。大人帮小孩子梳洗、吃饭和穿衣的时间要比北美人想象的长得多。在中国文化里，团体精神也要比独立重要得多了。假期的时候，人们也比较喜欢去人多、热闹的地方而不愿意去躲起来。"热闹"这个词很难翻译成英文，更难翻译成一个有好意的词，因为这个词里包含着热热闹闹、吵吵闹闹、有很多人的意思。中国社会没有北美社会那么平等。权威和个别的权威人物是要尊敬的，不该批评，更不该公开地批评。孩子应该尊重和听从长辈和父母。近年来，因为"一个孩子好"政策，大家都担心一代代的孩子会被宠坏，会有不好的行为，也非常担心大人会被孩子指挥着。

人 际 关 系

在北美，一般来说，人际关系不是最重要的。当然人际关系有时候也很有用,但并不是一般人随时都想利用的。人们在找工作和商业交易的时候不太喜欢靠关系做事,要不然会显得自己没有能力。一般人觉得最重要的是要靠自己的本事做事。再者,一般的人也不一定会期望友谊是特别长久的;友谊的长久常会取决于相互之间的兴趣和利益。同一个学校毕业并不一定是朋友。同事只是在一起工作的人,也不一定非做朋友不可。到中学和大学的时候,老师和学生会接近平等,平等说话,甚至互相只用名字称呼。而且,毕业以后,师生关系也不一定会保留得特别长久。

但是在中国,相比之下,人际关系在社会上向来都比较重要。有社会关系和没有社会关系会在找工作、孩子能上什么学校、商业交易是否能顺利进行等方面产生很大的作用。而且人们一般都不会觉得利用关系是不对或不好的事。中国人的友谊,至少在理想上,是应该长久的。同学和同事差不多必定会变成朋友。学生总是应该向老师表示敬意,而且毕业以后,师生关系应该是长久保持的。

直爽与含蓄

在北美,有一个交流的规则,就是"直截了当",说话别"拐弯抹角"。特别是在谈判交易的时候,一般都得清楚并直接地说话。人们直接说要说的话,不拐弯抹角地说。虽然加拿大人和美国人也讲究面子,可是面子并不是交往中主要考虑的事。况且,人们不会特别想到要给对方面子。人与人之间有时会产生冲突和争执,可是人们不一定会将此看成坏事。不但如此,他们会认为冲突和争执反而会产生意想不到的好效果。同时,大家也不一定会觉得伤感情。

在中国社会里,一般的交流规则是清楚而不过于率直。在交流这方面,面子是很重要的。谁都不应该让人没面子或丢脸。不但如此,甚至要能给人面子;若是能让别人在同辈或同事间站得住脚并抬得起头,那就更是锦上添花了。如果这样,这个被给予面子的人有朝一日也会还礼的。一般来说,冲突和争执式的直截了当的说法是不受欢迎的,因为这样会伤感情,也会叫人丢脸。因此,有时候有冲突性的意见得间接地表达出来，或者请第三者来传达。那就是说，有时得听字里行间的意思和第三者的意见。

进餐与座位

在加拿大和美国，正式进餐的桌子是长方形的。男主人和女主人分别坐在长方桌的两端。男主客坐在女主人的右边，女主客坐在男主人的右边。其他的客人可以随便坐，可是最好是一男一女。一般由男主人或女主人安排座位，客人等到座位决定好后才坐下。每人面前都已摆好一份碗盘和一份刀叉等。通常用的桌布和餐巾都是白色的。一般吃饭时禁忌将碗盘端起来，吃喝的时候也不能出声。喝汤喝到碗底的时候也不可以把碗端起来，而要把汤碗向外倾斜，再用汤匙把汤盛起来喝。饭菜来的时候，就会传来传去，客人可以自己多拿或少拿。可是最好把自己拿到自己盘子里的饭菜都吃完。在外面吃饭的时候，有人会决定"各付各的账"。要是如此，那么点菜前会告诉服务员饭后给每个人各自的账单，每个人也要自己负责给小费。

正式的中餐桌是圆的。男主人对着门坐，第一主客坐在他的右边，第二主客坐在他的左边。女主人对着男主人坐，有时候第二主客可以坐在她的右边。吃中

图4　西方正式餐具的摆法　李盈作

图5 正式中餐桌的摆法 李盈作

餐时客人坐在主人右边是有一定意义的:因为这样主人给客人夹菜会容易一点。主人给客人夹菜是有礼貌的表现。有时候,主人方的人和客人数目一样多,那么每一主人方的人旁边就座一位客人,以便主人方照顾每一位客人。中餐桌的坐法不一定是一男一女。有时是男的挨着坐在一起,女的挨着坐在一起,有人说这是为了便于谈话。正式请客时,最好是用红色或金黄色的桌布和餐巾。共用的菜饭放在旋转桌上,就不必将很重的大盘碗端起来。小饭碗和汤碗可以端起来以方便吃饭和喝汤。有些人甚至于喝汤时出声,也不算没礼貌,因为喝汤时吸汤也可以使热汤凉一点,以便喝下。主人让过几次菜以后,客人也可以自己夹菜。桌上会有公筷和公匙供大家用来夹菜和盛汤。如在外面吃饭,一般都由请客的人付账,但大家还是会抢一下账单。没付钱的人一般会回请。在一般的情况下,中国人不会各付各的账。

礼 物

在访问加拿大和美国时,来访的人都应该带交换的礼物,如大型画册、全国或各省或各城市的风景画册等。礼物可以是上面有国徽、省徽、校徽或公司徽章的各种礼物,也可以是代表性的工艺美术品等。在加拿大和美国,其他给礼物的情况有：被请去别人家作客、过生日、婚礼或圣诞节等。要是被请去别人家作客吃饭，一般可以带花、巧克力糖或一瓶酒等。生日和圣诞节的礼物都是给个人的，所以要看人看情况而给。婚礼时的礼物通常都是可以帮助新婚夫妇成家的东西，如床单、厨房用具、碗盘、桌布等。通常不会给钱，可是可以给礼券，新婚夫妇可以拿礼券去买所需的东西。婚礼的礼物是不当着客人面打开的。圣诞节的礼物要到圣诞节那天才能打开。其他的礼物一般都是当面就打开看并致谢的。到别人家里做客时给的礼物，如果是花，主人通常会摆出来与大家共赏；如果是糖或酒，主人就会拿出来与大家共尝。

在中国，交换礼物是必要的礼仪，尤其是正式的访问。交换的礼物也与加拿大和美国的相类似，但中方的礼物有时更为贵重。中国人请客通常在外边而不在家里。可以给请客的主人们礼物，但通常多用回请的方式。春节的时候，长者会给孩子们和年轻人红包。长者过生日，通常都由晚辈请客庆祝。给新婚夫妇的礼物通常是红包里装钱。忌讳给的礼物包括钟、手帕，也不给已婚的男人送绿帽子。亲自送礼物时，应有礼貌地用双手奉上。一般接受者不把包好的礼物在送礼的人面前打开。

迎接与送别

在北美，迎接和送别相当友善，但比中国人要随便得多。如果去办公室或者人家里拜访，通常人们不会很正式地迎接客人。也许会给客人挂一下大衣和帽子等。客人走的时候也不会特意把客人送出门口，特别是还有别的客人在的时候。主人一般只给客人开门，而客人自行离去。

可是在中国，人们对礼仪式的迎接和送别是很重视的。在办公室，当拜访人离开的时候，被拜访的人一定要有礼貌地送客出门。如果是在家里，当拜访人离开的时候，主人一定要送客出门，甚至送到车边、汽车站或火车站。无论如何，总得送一段路，才算有礼貌。只在门口看着客人离去是很不礼貌的。

对年龄的态度

在北美社会，重点经常都放在充满活力的年轻人身上。人们，尤其是妇女，不喜欢别人问自己的年龄。因为年龄的大小被视为自己的事，别人管不着的。谁也不会主动告诉新认识的人自己的年龄，因为用英文谈话比较平等，不必刻意用什么敬语或改变态度。有些人甚至觉得问女人年龄是不礼貌的。而且这样的问题常使女人处于难于应付的地位，不知照实回答好，还是不回答好。在一个注重年轻人的社会里，很多老人都怕老，怕"没用了"人家就不尊敬自己了。因之，老年人一般不爱认老，而且对能比较独立、能自食其力而感到骄傲。有一次，在一个国际会议上，中方代表为了要感谢一位年纪较大的女组织人，他说："……她年纪已经这么大了……"翻译员也就照样翻译了。所有的人都大笑起来，因为这样说是非常不客气的。而中方本来的用意却是为了表示敬意。又有一次，一个中国留学生站在一位年纪较大的妇女后面等车。公共汽车来的时候，这位妇女费力地上车。留学生主动伸手去扶她。没想到，她反而回过头来大声向他说："我还没那么老呢！"

在中国，大部分人常会主动告诉别人自己的年龄，也会问别人的年龄。只是近年来，城市里年轻女性不喜欢别人问她的年龄。一般四十几岁的人就常说自己老了。有时也不一定是颓丧的意思。对中国人来说，年纪大的人富有经验和知识，所以是值得尊敬的。同时，大家应该尽量帮助他们，包括在车上给他们让座。20世纪80年代的时候，北京的公共汽车上明显地写着："文明车，请让座给老、残、孕、外"。西方人看到这个标语里有"外"，总是很吃惊，又觉得很可笑。小孩子和年轻人要叫年纪大的人"爷爷"和"奶奶"，叫"老头儿"和"老太太"是非常没有礼貌的。

感谢与道歉

　　加拿大人非常客气。加拿大人经常都在说"谢谢！"和"对不起！"甚至对亲朋好友也不时表示感谢和道歉。有个笑话说，有人撞了加拿大人，加拿大人还说："对不起！"其实是应该由撞他的人说"对不起"的。很多人也说加拿大人是很自谦的。有个笑话说：加拿大人要听见别人夸奖他，他一定会回头去看是不是在夸奖他后面的人！总之，北美人常说"谢谢！"和"对不起！"对熟人和家人也不例外。否则，人们会认为这个人很没有礼貌。

　　中国人也常说"谢谢"和"对不起"，但是并不是在任何情况下都说的，向熟悉的人和自己的家人表示感谢和道歉就会觉得不太亲近。所以，感谢常是用脸上的表情和回报来表达。北美人和中国人用"谢谢"一词，有显著的差异。比如，要有人夸奖一位女士的衣服或帽子很漂亮的时候，加拿大人或美国人会说："啊，谢谢！"可是，中国人就会谦虚地说："哪里！哪里！"

象 征 意 义

颜　色

颜色不只是美丽，也有实用的价值。譬如说，世界各地都利用颜色符号来传达特别的或重要的信息。不同的文化甚至对不同的颜色联想不同的意义以表达各种不同的感情，如喜悦、悲哀、愤怒、嫉妒或爱情。这些差异反映着文化传统的差异，不同的文化对颜色及其联想会有相当的差异。其实，即使在同一文化中，利用颜色符号来传达的信息在不同历史时期或地点也会有所不同。北美和中国对颜色的象征性常会有相当大的差异。虽然现代社会由于信息的交流观点常有趋同现象，但某些差异还是较大的，其所表现的文化特点也是值得注意的。

在北美：

- 黑色：黑色是夜晚和黑暗的颜色，隐藏着罪恶，然而又是权利和世故的颜色。黑色也是葬礼的颜色，表示哀悼和庄重。一般来说，黑色是很正式的颜色。在很正式的场合，人们主要穿黑色的晚礼服或西装。结婚典礼时新郎和伴郎都穿黑色礼服。有一种叫"黑领带"的餐会，是非常正式的餐会。人们，特别是男士，一定穿黑礼服，打黑领带。与黑色有关的说法包括：黑色喜剧，是用悲哀的事件排成喜剧；黑名单；（黑色）敲诈；黑市；"黑羊"是指不成器的孩子和害群之马；黑色星期五，曾是股票市场倒闭之日。

现今，指美国感恩节后的第一天（十一月第四个星期五），此日商店都大减价，所以收入"黑字"。加拿大有些大公司现亦随之。

- 蓝色：蓝色是晴空和平静的海的颜色，象征着和平、平静和纯洁，但是也与悲哀和颓丧有关。英语说"蓝色情感"就是悲哀的意思。蓝色是最受欢迎的颜色，因为人们对蓝色有一种安全感。蓝色也是男婴儿衣物的颜色。通俗的用法有：蓝色血统，是说有贵族的血统；所谓"蓝色的电影"却是中文所指的黄色电影；蓝色月亮，表明不常发生的事；英语的"蓝空霹雳"就是中文所说的晴空霹雳。

- 绿色：绿色是大自然的颜色，象征春天、繁殖力、青春和希望；也代表嫉妒；又表示环保，如"绿化"；也代表安全，如绿灯。如果说给一个人或一件事开绿灯，就是说可以进行了；也是美国钞票的别称，叫"绿背"；又代表缺乏经验，如果说一个人有点绿，就是说这个人没有经验、天真又容易受骗；如果说一个人有绿色大拇指，就是说此人很会种植东西；要形容一个人嫉妒或要生病，也用绿色来形容。

- 粉红色：粉红色象征着浪漫、爱情和温和。因其代表温和，所以可以降低暴力。这是一般给女婴儿选礼物的颜色。"相当粉红"这个词是用来非正式地说一个人身体很健康、精神也很好；粉红条子，是撤职的通知；逗得发粉红色，是说挺高兴的。

- 红色：红色是血的颜色，象征着生命和活力。因此，红色也代表强烈的感情和力量。红色容易引起注意，也表示危险，用来指示禁止，如红灯就是要停止的意思。红色的用法包括：赤字；脸红；红旗表示危险；红色地毯是用来欢迎贵宾的；"红色警惕"是在觉到危险和紧急事件时发出的信号；"看见红色"是说生气的意思。

- 白色：白色象征纯洁和干净。新娘的婚礼服是白色的，婚礼时也用白花，都代表纯洁；医生常穿白色以示洁净；有白色木头矮围墙的房子表示家庭安详、幸福；白色圣诞，表示下雪的圣诞节；白色大象是说对主人已没什么价值的东西；举白旗是投降的意思；白色谎言，是为了客气而不太关紧要的谎言；当然还有白色恐怖。
- 黄色：黄色是太阳的颜色，象征着乐观。黄色也是容易引起注意的颜色。北美的出租汽车和带学生的校车常是黄色的。黄色还是警告的颜色，表示有危险，比如说："黄色的警戒"。黄色的交通灯表示要小心，灯快要变红了。黄色在非正式的情形下也象征胆怯。比如，可以说一个人是黄色，就是说这个人很胆小。黄色新闻是指新闻报道特别耸人听闻。

在中国：

- 黑色：并不是好颜色，代表黑夜、黑暗和哀悼。人们穿黑色衣服、戴黑色袖圈以示哀悼；逝世的人的照片上围着黑布；公布名单时，已逝世者名字外边要有黑框。用"黑"字的词有：黑心、黑手党、黑市、黑话和黑客。颜色也与物件、方向和季节有关。在五方象征系统里，黑色代表北方、水和冬季。
- 蓝色：如一句歇后语所说："外国人看戏——蓝了眼儿了，"就是说惊讶，也有焦急的意思。"蓝桥"是情人相会的地方的比喻。
- 金色：金色是吉祥的颜色，象征着高贵、富裕和荣誉。中国人特别喜欢金子和金色，也特别喜欢佩戴黄金饰物。金色也代表皇帝和皇家。用"金"字的词包括：金榜题名、金玉满堂等。
- 绿色：绿色是大自然的颜色，一般说是好颜色。碧玉代表美丽、幸福和美德。现在绿色变成绿色环境和环保的颜色，如绿化。"绿色食物"是指安全的有机食物。但是一个结婚的男人"戴绿帽子"却不是好事。绿色代表东方、植物和春季。
- 粉红色：因受西方的影响，粉红色象征着爱情。
- 红色：对中国人来说，这是最吉祥的颜色、是所有吉祥喜庆的颜色，如婚礼和新年。新娘穿红色衣服，新郎也戴红花。现在，在大城市，因受西方的影响，新娘也穿好看的白色婚礼服。新婚夫妇的新房有很多红色，如红色被褥。红色是新年时最重要的颜色：孩子穿红衣服，拿红包。还有红色对联、红色剪纸、红色鞭炮等。红色代表南方、火和夏季。
- 白色：一般来说，白色是不祥的颜色。白色历来是死亡和丧事的颜色，是戴孝的颜色。但近年来，吊丧时也常用黑色来代替。因受西方习惯的影响，新娘有时也穿西方的白色婚礼服。"白玉无瑕"表示完美无缺。白色代表西方、金属和秋天。
- 黄色：黄色是重要的颜色，代表权力和权威，也是皇帝的颜色：皇帝穿黄色，坐黄色宝座。黄色电影和黄色杂志都是与色情有关的。黄泉，指地下、坟地。黄色代表中央和土地。

数　　字

数字在不同的文化里有不同的意义。有些数字被视为是吉利的，因为传统上认为这些数字有"吉利的力量"，而另一些数字却被看成不吉利的，因为代表着霉气。有些北美人嘲笑这些所谓的迷信，但他们却不愿意车牌里有"666"；有些中国人当众否认这类迷信，可是会花大价钱买有吉利数字的车牌。换句话说，北美人和中国人也许相信的吉利的数字不同，但都会对数字有一种看法。

北美文化里：

- "3"在民间文学以及神话和宗教里都很重要。在民间故事里，主角总是有三个机会猜谜语，猜到后才能实现其愿望。或者要完成三件事，才能得到奖赏。打棒球时，打击手只有三次机会击球。生命有三个环节：出生、生活与死亡。在基督教里，上帝是神圣的三位一体：父、子和圣灵。人体包含着三部分：身体、头脑和灵魂。谚语有：第三次很灵；好事成三。时间有三段：过去、现在和未来。三角有正面的意思，指金字塔形的力量，又有负面的意思，指三角恋爱。物质有三个"王国"：动物王国、植物王国和矿物王国。
- "7"被很多北美人认为是很吉利的数字。在赌双筛骨的时候，"7"是第一次投筛时赢的数字。广义地看，"7"一直被看成一个完整或整体的数字，如：七个海洋代表全世界，古代是指地中海、亚得里亚海、黑海、红海、里海、阿拉伯海和波斯湾；现代是指北大西洋、南大西洋、北太平洋、南太平洋、印度洋、南冰洋和北冰洋。天文学里有7个原始行星：太阳、月亮、水星、金星、火星、木星和土星。它们代表着整个太阳系。"7"还代表：一星期有7天，代表造物的7天；虹的7彩，代表整个光谱：红、橙、黄、绿、蓝、靛、紫；七重天和七层地狱；音符有7个。
- "10"象征完美和完整，也常用来表示满分，如"十分之十"。
- "13"是不吉利的数字。有些楼房不标示13层楼或13号房间，也没有人要住在地址是13的房子里。阿波罗13号是美国唯一不成功、未达到月球的火箭。13是不吉利的数字，因为耶稣最后晚餐时有13个人，就是耶稣和他的12个信徒，信徒中的犹大背叛了耶稣。据说绞架的梯子有13个阶梯。当任何月份的13号又碰上星期五，很多人便把它看成很不吉利的日子，因为耶稣是星期五受的刑。
- "666"：6本身对北美的人没什么意义，可是多数人都会认为"666"是代表反基督者、魔王。说出或者写出"666"就是叫魔王的方法，即"叫魔王，魔王就出现了。"有些人认为"666"非常不吉利，如果地址、公寓、电话号码或者车牌里有这个数字，他们是一定不要的。

中国文化里：

在中国文化里，数字和数字的象征也相当重要，而且常常与同音字有关。奇数是阳数，偶数是阴数。除了4以外，人们在许多场合都比较喜欢偶数。比如，人们常选偶数日子结婚，而不喜欢奇数的日子。
- "1"表示整体、完整和一体。"一心一意"表示全心全意地对人或对事。

"一"也是生万物的开端。但有些人把它看成不太好的数字，因为它代表独处和孤单。

- "2"是好数字，因为有"成双"的意思。无论是事情或人，能成双成对都是好的，所以结婚是双喜。同时，人们也常说：好事成双。

- "3"是好数字，指天地人的合一。老子说："一生二，二生三，三生万物。"根据传统的看法，宇宙包括三大类：天、地、人。中国有三教：儒家、道家、佛家。幸福的生活要有三样：福、禄、寿。含有"三"字的说法也不少：三思而行；三心二意；三省吾身；三天打鱼，两天晒网；三个臭皮匠，抵得上一个诸葛亮等。

- "4"是不吉利的数字，因为听起来像"死"。很多中国人尽量避免与4有关。很多楼房不提4楼；旅馆或公寓也没有4号房间。可是，"4"并非一向都是不吉利的数字。传统上有四喜：福、禄、寿、喜；四神兽：朱鸟、白虎、青龙、乌龟。四种有德的植物：梅、兰、竹、菊。人生的四喜是：久旱逢甘雨、他乡遇故知、洞房花烛夜、金榜题名时。另外，佛家说的"四大皆空"的四大是：地、水、火、风。当然还有四季：指春、夏、秋、冬。有"四"字的说法也不少，包括：四面八方、四通八达、四分五裂、四海为家、四海之内皆兄弟等。

- "5"在有些人看来不好，因为听起来像"无"，所以商业方面的人不太喜欢这个数字。与5有关的还有：五行——水、火、土、木、金；五谷——麻、黍、稷、麦、菽；五福——长寿、富贵、康宁、好德、善终；五毒——蝎子、蛇、壁虎、蜈蚣、蟾蜍。还有些与"五"有关的词：五花八门、五颜六色、五谷丰登、五彩缤纷、五味俱全、五体投地等。

- "6"是好数字，因为听起来像"禄"。有六亲：父子、兄弟、夫妻；六畜：牛、马、羊、鸡、狗、猪。佛家说的"六根清净"的"六根"是眼、耳、鼻、舌、身、意；道家说的"六神无主"的"六神"是指主宰人的心、肺、肝、肾、脾、胆的神灵；儒家的六艺是：礼、乐、射、御、书、数。

- "7"在有些人看来不好，因为听起来像"弃"。但是也有许多并非负面的与

"7"有关的，如：七仙女、竹林七贤（阮籍、嵇康、山涛、刘伶、阮咸、向秀、王戎）。还有七情。佛教指的是：喜、怒、忧、惧、爱、憎、欲；儒家指的是：喜、怒、哀、惧、爱、恶、欲。另外又有开门7件事：柴、米、油、盐、酱、醋、茶。

- "8"是特别好的数字，因为听起来像发财的"发"，是很多人追求的数字。据说，"8"与佛教也有关，因为莲花有八瓣。中国文化里有"八仙过海，各显其能"。传说的"八仙"是：汉钟离、张果老、吕洞宾、铁拐李、曹国舅、韩湘子、蓝采和、何仙姑。生辰八字也是很重要的。人们对楼房、房间、车牌、电话和手机号码都希望求到、买到有"8"字的。2008年奥运会的开幕时间是：2008年8月8日下午8点8分8秒！
- "9"是好数字，因为它是单数里最大的"阳"数，又因为听起来像"久"所以代表永久和长寿。皇帝跟"九"有着密切的关系。皇帝的袍上有九龙，北京的北海还有代表皇帝权力的九龙壁。紫禁城里有九千九百九十九间半房间。神话里说到"后羿射日"：原来天上有十个太阳，人们无法忍受其晒。后羿射掉了九个太阳，剩下现在的一个太阳，才使世界适宜人们居住。
- "10"象征全面或完整。中文里有许多用"十"字的说法，如十分、十足、十全和十全十美。
- 另外，还有与数字有关的好的说法：一帆风顺，二龙腾飞，三阳开泰，四季平安，五福临门，六六大顺，七星高照，八方来财，九九同心，十全十美，百事亨通，千事吉祥，万事如意！

动物与鸟类

北美文化中：

- 驴：驴是驮物的动物，但也因固执和不听支使有名。因之，便成了顽强、故持己见者的比喻,也常用来比喻愚笨、讨厌或可恶的人。
- 海狸:海狸是非常勤奋的筑坝的动物,常用来比喻忙碌而勤奋的人。口语里常说:"某人忙得像海狸一样。"海狸也是代表加拿大的动物。
- 鸽子:鸽子是温顺的鸟。传统上用来代表精神上的事物和灵魂,近年来都用它象征和平、爱好和平者和和平精神。通常与爱好战争的雕相对比。
- 老鹰:象征力量。白头鹰代表美国,象征独立精神。白头鹰左爪抓着箭(象征战争),右爪抓着橄榄枝叶(象征和平),表现着求和平的欲望,但也会以武力来保护和平。
- 狐狸:在北美,狐狸象征精明、狡猾、诡计多端。"狐狸"或"像狐狸"两词在北美已成为描写性感的人,特别是女性的词。"母狐狸"一词常用来描写美丽而有诱惑性的女子,几乎相当于描写女子为狐狸精。但是,北美并没有像中国民间故事中的狐狸精。
- 雕:在古代的埃及,雕象征灵魂;但在现代的北美表示好战,代表掠夺和剥夺别人利益的卑鄙的人。这可能是因为雕是一种食肉的鸟类,常扑食小动物。
- 狮子:狮子是"万兽之王",象征着权力和凶猛,常与胆小、纯洁的羔羊对比。
- 猫头鹰:猫头鹰代表智慧,也许是因为猫头鹰有能力预测天气,同时,在

图6　海狸　李盈作

图7　猫头鹰　李盈作

夜晚可以看得很清楚，又因为猫头鹰黑夜猎食小动物，所以人们把它看成黑夜的鸟，也与死亡相关。同时，有人也将木制猫头鹰放在屋顶上以驱逐鸟类和鼠类，并辟邪。

- 凤：西方的凤也是一只神话中的鸟，但不像中国的凤凰那么美丽。这个凤与太阳有关，像太阳每日重新升起一样，凤也会从死灰中复生。
- 老鼠：大老鼠常常与作恶有关，所以用来比喻令人讨厌、欺骗和不忠实的人。小老鼠常用来代表胆怯。
- 鹳鸟：因为鹳鸟坚贞而且育幼时间长，所以人们将之看作多产和好运的象征。在北美，父母常告诉小孩子，婴儿是由鹳鸟口中叼着个小包袱送来的，犹如麒麟送子。
- 鹫：这种鸟吃动物的尸体，故用来比喻欺凌、剥削弱小的人和掠夺、剥夺别人利益的卑鄙的人。英文俗语中有"文化鹫"一词，可指对文化事物和活动极有兴趣的人。

图8　死灰中复生的凤　李盈作

图9　鹳鸟送子　李盈作

中国文化中：

- 蝙蝠：在欧美的传统中，蝙蝠代表祸害与恶事。然而在中国，蝙蝠却代表祝福和好运，象征祝福和幸运。因为"蝠"与"福"同音。装饰等物上常有五只蝙蝠出现，就是"五福"的意思，代表长寿、幸运、健康、美德和寿终正寝。红蝙蝠更是吉利，因为"红"与"洪"同音，所以代表"洪福"。

- 鹤：鹤在画中或装饰品上代表长寿，而且常与松树同时出现，表示"松鹤延年"。有时也与石头或龟同时出现，更是寿上加寿。
- 鹿："鹿"与"禄"同音，所以用来比喻富裕和好运。
- 鸽子：鸽子代表忠诚和长寿，也许是因为鸽子是终身伴侣，而且公、母鸽子都会饲养小鸽子。在现代，鸽子也是和平的象征。
- 龙：中国的龙与西方的不同。中国的龙长而细，没有翅膀，而有爪子，也不像西方的龙那样喷火。中国的龙是仁慈的神话动物，有旱灾和火灾的时候会喷水救灾，象征着权势。如果爪子上有五个脚趾，则象征皇帝；如果龙与凤凰在一起，则象征皇帝与皇后。现在，龙也是中国和中国人以及权力的象征。
- 鱼：是财富和富裕的象征。"鱼"与"余"同音，"有鱼"有如"有余"，即绰绰有余，意味着"吉庆有余"。
- 狐狸：如同在西方一样，狐狸象征着狡猾。但在中国民间故事中，狐狸会成精，母狐狸精会诱惑书生等。
- 凤凰：雄为凤，雌为凰。在古代，人们认为如有此神话中的美丽鸟出现，就表示治理天下的君主是贤明的。凤凰与龙在一起，代表皇帝与皇后，也代表和谐的夫妇，即"龙凤呈祥"。
- 麒麟：关于这种神话中的动物样子的说法不一。一说麒麟是鹿的身子，牛尾巴，有鱼鳞，蹄子像马，是分裂的。雄的称麒，有一只角，雌的称麟，没有角。麒麟象征着太平和福寿，在太平盛世和有圣人时出现。麒麟是灵兽，也与多子有关。所谓"麒麟送子"，有如北美人认为的鹳鸟送子。
- 老虎：老虎在中国是万兽之王，象征力量、勇气和勇敢。人们相信老虎能镇邪，所以常有老虎塑像守坟。

图10　凤凰　李盈作

图11　麒麟　李盈作

- 龟：因为龟很长寿，所以一直是长寿的象征。又因为龟的壳是圆的，代表天，肚底是平的，代表地，所以是宇宙的代表，含有宇宙的机密。
- 鸳鸯：雄为鸳，雌为鸯。人们认为鸳鸯是终身伴侣，永不分离，所以是相亲相爱、忠贞不移的美好象征。
- 十二生肖：在传统的中国文化中，每12年为一周期；12年的每一年都由一种动物代表，依次为：鼠、牛、虎、兔、龙、蛇、马、羊、猴、鸡、狗和猪。每一生肖的动物都有其特征，人们认为会影响那年出生人的性格。

花卉与植物

北美文化中：

- 康乃馨（石竹）：粉红色的象征感恩，白色的象征纪念。母亲节时（五月的第二个星期日），孩子送给母亲石竹花。母亲还健在的，戴红花；母亲过世的，则戴白花。黄色康乃馨表示愉悦。

- 雏菊：在北美，白雏菊象征着天真无邪、质朴、纯洁和忍耐。人们认为它会为人的生活带来阳光。
- 勿忘我：送此花的人象征性地提醒接受花的人别忘了他或她。
- 罂粟花：此花代表复活和永生，因为罂粟花从不死亡，每年谢了又会复生。红色的罂粟花也象征流血牺牲。因之，在加拿大，每年的阵亡将士纪念日（11月11日）和美国的退伍军人节（11月11日）和阵亡将士纪念日（5月31日）期间，退伍军人和纪念阵亡军人的人都戴罂粟花或自制的罂粟花。
- 芸香：这种常青枞树象征美德，因为有人相信它能驱除邪恶。芸香也是悲哀的象征。
- 玫瑰：玫瑰代表爱情和浪漫，特别是红玫瑰。在情人节（2月14日）和特殊场合，人们会给喜爱的人送玫瑰以示爱意。白玫瑰代表纯洁，红玫瑰象征热情，黄色的表示智慧和喜悦。玫瑰是美国的国花。

图12 勿忘我 李盈作　　图13 罂粟花 李盈作　　图14 芸香 李盈作

中国文化中：

- 竹子：竹子象征忍耐性、强劲、正直和柔韧灵活性，这是因为竹子四季常青、能伸能屈，而且很快就能恢复到直立的位子。人们还常用竹子来比喻正直的君子。
- 菊花：菊花盛开于秋季，象征长寿和忍耐性。
- 荷花：荷花盛开于夏季，出污泥而不染，故为清高、纯洁的象征。
- 兰花：自古以来，人们都把兰花视为典雅、高洁、坚贞不渝和不屈不挠人格的象征。兰花、梅花、菊花和竹子被称为"四君子"。兰花更是常被称为"花中真君子"，向来为高雅、忠贞的人士所爱。
- 牡丹：此花为万花之后，代表富贵荣华。
- 松树：松树是岁寒三友（松、竹、梅）之一。因为松树是常青树，而且可以活很久。所以，松树象征着耐性、长寿和忠诚。
- 梅花：梅花代表美丽和温顺，这是因为此花美丽而娇俏。而且，梅花在严冬时开花，所以它还象征忍耐力，并带来春天将至的信息。

体态语与手势

体　态　语

　　在任何沟通行为中，非语言的暗示（即行动的上下文）所含的意义常会比语言本身（也即口头上的内容）更丰富。比如：说英语、法语和说西班牙语的人，虽然都说英文，但可能会在体态语的规范和期望上有相当大的差异。说英语的人和说中文的人的体态与规范常会有更大一点的差异，如果不了解，也许会产生误会。

身距

　　两个说同一语言的人在谈话的时候会不知不觉地自动协调出并保持身体之间正常的距离。我们不知不觉地都会对在公开场合、社交、个人交流和亲切关系交流时应该有的和保持的距离有一定的期望。
　　一般在加拿大和美国，无论是等公共汽车、排队买票或排队付钱的时候，人与人之间的距离都会大些、疏散些。然而，在中国，在同样的情况下，人与人之间的距离就会小一点、挤一点。加拿大人或美国人在中国排队，可能就会有人插队，因为中国人会认为这个外国人没在排队。相反，中国人在加拿大或美国排队，加拿大或美国人就会觉得这个人不太礼貌，离人这么近，侵入了个人拥有的空间。

浩尔（E. T. Hall）在1966年的作品《隐藏的尺寸》（*The Hidden Dimension*）中谈到，在一般情况下，北美说英语的人交流时，按不同的情况，其大致距离如下：
- 亲密：18英寸（46厘米）
- 个人：18英寸至4英尺（46厘米至1.2米）
- 社交：4至12英尺（1.2米至3.6米)
- 公共距离：12至25英尺（3.6米至7.6米)

图15　谈话时，不熟的人身距较远　李盈作　　图16　谈话时，较熟悉的人身距较近　李盈作

因为中国人向来比较群体化，个人主义不很强，所以中国人谈话时人与人之间的平均距离比北美人之间的要小。中国人一般好像比较能忍受较近的距离。但男女之间的身距会大一点。在比较挤的汽车或火车上，中国人就不会觉得像北美人那么不舒服。

眼光的接触

对加拿大人和美国人来说，眼光的接触是很重要的，因为这样才能表现诚实和中肯，其含义是："我开诚布公。"相反，盯着人看，甚至于盯着看陌生人，却是不礼貌的举止。与人谈话时完全不看人就有无聊、不感兴趣、不高兴、羞耻或甚至于心虚感。对着人家挤一只眼睛表示调情、友善或者觉得有趣，甚至于表示所说的话只是开玩笑，不认真。

图17　眼光接触握手紧表现中肯　李盈作　　图18　躲避眼光，不直视　李盈作

中国人说话时保持眼光接触也表示诚实和中肯，但是也要小心，不要不断地保持眼光的接触，以免显得"咄咄逼人"。如果是男女之间接触或谈话，更是需要不时躲避眼光。这种情景表示谦虚、害羞或者不是以眼光逼人。通常，上级对下级或长者对年轻人可以不断地看着对方而不是不礼貌。挤一只眼睛是不太礼貌的，一般不这么做。

人际交流的协调

在北美，开会时，由主席先发言。在座参加会议的人可以顺次发言，或者谁有话要说就先说。通常谈话的时候并没有一定谁先说谁后说的次序，有话要说的人就说。一般独占说话机会是不礼貌的，但如有话要打岔，就先说一句"对不起"就可以说了。要是两个人同时说话，则说："抱歉！"或"对不起！"之后，一方就请另一方先说。走路、进门或出门的时候总是"女士优先"，并不管地位高低或年岁的大小。几个人一起走路的时候，步调应该相合。

在中国，开会时，由主席先发言，接下去一般都有发言的次序。通常谈话时，大家总是让上级或年长者先说，其他的人听着。插嘴是不礼貌的。走路、进门或出门的时候，大家总会请上级或年长者先走，而不论上级或年长者是男或是女。

触摸

在北美，握手很普通。新认识的人要握手，很久不见面的朋友见面也会握手。握手一般要紧，以表诚意。为了客气，男的一般等女方先伸手才握手。好朋友见面和道别常会拥抱。在公共场合亲吻，或更常见的是吻面颊，在加拿大会比在中国常见。然而，在这方面，加拿大人要比美国人保守一点。

新认识的中国人通常只问候"你好""幸会"等。然而，因受西方的影响，现在很多人也握手。但中国人握手不会像加拿大人和美国人那么紧，特别是男女握手。这并不表示不诚意，而只是新认识的人之间触摸握手感觉不太自然。陌生的男女之间握手会有点不太好意思。相反，同性别之间倒常见有人拉手或挽着手臂走路，特别是年轻和年纪大的人之间，以示友好。

静默

虽然传统上在北美一直教小孩子"沉默是金"，但要是在会议或者谈话时有较长的一段沉默的时间的话，大多数人都会觉得有点尴尬。要是谈话时有静默的时间，有个空隙，则有人赶快会想出什么来说，以免冷场，只为了能把空隙填上。这一方面是加拿大人和美国人把流利的口才看成美德；另一方面，沉默可能表现"我们之间无话可说"。在大集会上，有人演说，或者有演出上演时，大家就会自动安静下来，以表示尊敬演讲者、演出者和其他在场的人。

大多数的中国人在会议或谈话时比加拿大人或美国人更能忍受较长的静默时间。在会议或谈话时如有一段沉静的时间，大家不会急着去填那沉静的空隙。

这段安静的时间可供人深思所说的话或者反思其意义，没人会在沉静时感到尴尬。有时候中国人用沉静和不言语来说"没有""不可以"或者"不成"等。因为"没有""不可以""不成"或者"没意见"等字眼是对抗性的，所以许多人就以不言语来回答，以避免冲突。虽然如此，一般中国人都是很和睦、合群的。所以有时候在集会和有人演讲的时候，特别是在庆典的时候，很多人会聊天、交谈。

体态与手势

手势与体态语是人际交流时非常重要的一部分。手势也是体态语的一部分。手势和体态语都是与特定的文化联系在一起的。不同的动作在不同的语言和文化群里会有不同的意义，但其目的都是要表达意义，所以要了解其他文化的手势和体态才好达到互相了解的目的。

北美人的体态与手势

- 同意：上下点头表现同意、接受和示意认知。
- 虚吻：这是一种嘴做吻的样子，但嘴唇不与对方接触，是社交上象征性较亲密的表现。有时候，双方的脸可以接触，有时可做出像"姆哇"的声音。另外一种是飞吻，是两人距离远时做的。首先，亲一下自己的手掌，然后将亲过的地方向对方吹去。
- 愤怒或敌意：用拳头示意。有时会对要表示愤怒或敌意的人挥动拳头。抗议或不服气的时候，会握着拳头，双拳叉腰。
- 赞同：要表示赞同、感激或同意时，可以将大拇指向上翘，其他手指合着。要赞美别人事情做得

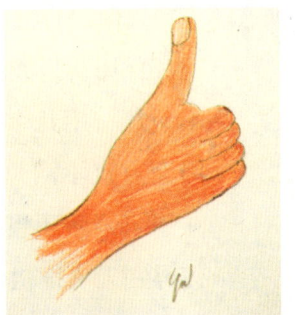

图19 北美人表示赞同的手势 李盈作

好，也可以用这个手势。这个手势也叫翘大拇指。另外表示赞同的方法是点几次头。

- 不好，不同意：大拇指朝下。这与翘大拇指刚好相反。
- 召唤：抬起手，手指向前，手心朝上，再将手指曲向自己的脸或身子几次；另一种方式是将食指抬起，手背对着对方，将食指不断向里外弯曲。后者较为随便。
- 无聊：感觉无聊，或者很困，或要表示时间不早了，可以用手遮住嘴，做打哈欠状。将两个大拇指靠近，平着，上下来回转动，也是表示很无聊。
- 不好意思：用一只手掌或两只手掌遮住脸，是表示不好意思、失望、受挫折或吃惊。
- 致候和迎接：致候和迎接时最普通的方式是握手。握手时一定要紧握对方的手，以示真诚的意思。但中国人会觉得握得太紧有过于亲热的感觉。另外较随便的致候就是点点头而已。

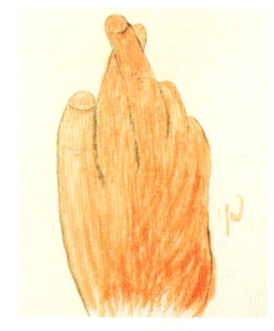

图20　北美人祈望好运的手势　李盈作

- 祈望好运：这个手势也称为"让我们交叉着指头"，意思是：希望一切顺利，祈望有好运。这个动作的做法是将中指交叉在食指之上，其他的指头和拇指合住。有时有人在说小谎或只口头答应什么事而并不想履行时，会把这个动作放在背后说话，意思是希望以后没有报应。
- "我"：用食指或大拇指指向自己的胸膛。
- 不耐烦：用几个指尖轮流敲东西表示别人在说话时想插嘴而还没有机会，因而有点不耐烦。这个动作也可能表示此人已不耐烦而想要离去。有时在想事情而还想不到解决的方法时，也会用手指敲东西。
- 侮辱别人（很粗俗）：中指向上伸出，其他手指合拢，手背朝着对方，有时甚至将前臂向上震动。这也叫做"给人指头"，是表现有意的侮辱、瞧不起或者不尊敬，是非常粗俗和猥亵的手势。一般来说，这是一个不可原谅的动作。有时为了方便，中国人也用中指指示，而北美人看到时不是吃惊，就是觉得非常可笑。
- "开玩笑呢"：表示自己说的话或做的事只是好玩儿或开玩笑而已，可以对着对方眨一下眼睛。这个动作又会被中国人误会成送秋波。
- 钱：表示钱或要钱，是用大拇指头来回地搓食指和拇指的尖端，是模仿数钞票的动作。
- "我不会告诉别人"：用食指和大拇指顺着嘴唇往一方拉，好像把拉链拉住一样。
- 不行、不好、不对、不：手臂伸出，手心朝外，对着对方，将手左右摇动，或者摇头两三次。摇头也可以表示"我不知道"或"我不懂"。另一种表示否定的动作是对着对方将食指左右摆动。
- 荒唐：用食指对着太阳穴在边上画圆圈是说荒唐、无聊、胡说或"你疯了"，有时是开玩笑用的。
- 好、可以：用食指和大拇指做个圈，其他三个手指伸直，手心朝外，表示好、可以、太好了、没问题等。
- 指：要指人或东西，就用食指指，其他手指合住。这不是不礼貌的动作。
- 迷惑：要是有点迷惑、怀疑、糊涂或不解，就用手抓头。
- 轻蔑：如果要表示轻视谁，就用大拇指指着自己的鼻子，其他手指来回转动，有时还会发出"呐、呐、呐、呐……"的声音。这个动作稍微粗俗些。
- 羞，羞：用一只食指在另一只食指上，对着目标人快速摸动几次，以示某人做错事或做羞辱

图21　侮辱别人的手势
李盈作

图22　"好"的手势
李盈作

的事。
- 请保持安静：要使人安静或别吵，只需将食指伸出，放在嘴前。有时此动作也伴有"嘘嘘……"的声音。
- 微笑：对人微笑是表示友善。可以对熟人微笑，也可以对陌生人微笑，以示友善。有时微笑表示同意或赞同。
- 团结：要表示团结一致，就把握拳的手，手背朝着自己，举过头高，甚至加上口号。
- 停住：将手臂一直伸出，手心对着要叫停住的人。
- 惊讶：将双眼大睁，眉毛向上挪动就表示很惊讶。
- 没关系、无所谓：要表示不确定、不知如何回答，或者要表示不在乎、没关系，就将双肩往上耸。有时伴以双手打开，手掌向上举的动作。
- 胜利的手势：用食指和中指做个"V"形，手心朝外，手臂举起。对有些人来说，如果手心朝内则是侮辱的手势。可是，有时候人们也根本不注意手心是朝内或朝外。
- "你好"和"再见"：手臂向外、向上伸出，手掌打开，整个手对着外面，向左右摆动，犹如反的钟摆。这个动作也可以用来吸引别人的注意力。较随便地说"再见！"的方式只是点点头。另外，在较为随便或距离较近的情况下，则将手伸出，手心朝下，手指上下摆动数次。
- 对、同意：点头可以表示很好和同意。

中国人的体态和手势：

中国人说话的时候通常不用很多手势。中国人觉得北美人多用手势和面部表情沟通，而中国人多是用语言沟通，脸上表情不很丰富。如果谁说话时用手势加重语气，人家就会说这个人"手舞足蹈"或者"比手画脚"。中国人一般不耸肩，也不作"好，okay"的手势，因为用大拇指和食指做个圈，很容易被人看成"0"的。对人伸出中指，不是无礼的手势。其实，有时候会看到中国人用中指指点或说"一",而不用食指。

- 同意:现在,很多人用竖起大拇指来表现同意、很好、了不起、真棒等意思。
- 召唤:手臂伸出,手心朝下,用手指向人上下摇动,有如抓动。召唤小孩或叫狗等时,是用伸出食指,再向自己弯动几次。
- 烦:觉得很烦或者不顺当的时候,有人会举起右手抓头。这个动作有时候表示不知如何是好。
- 数数:用手数数的时候,是这样数:

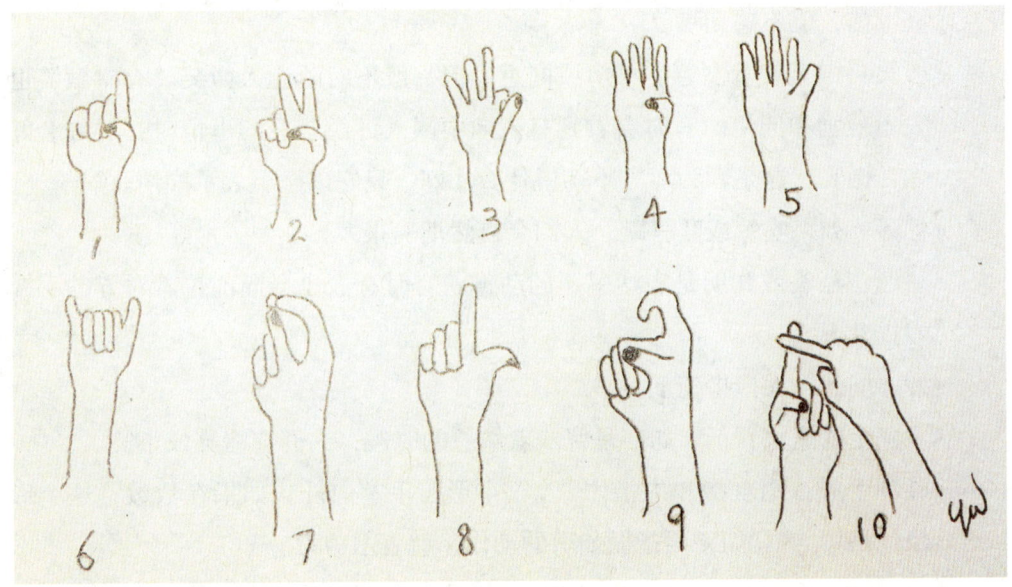

图23　中国人用手数1至10　李盈作

- 指方向:要是很忙或者手里拿着东西的时候,中国人常用下巴指点前、后、左、右。要用大拇指往下指是表示下面。
- 吃饭:要表示该吃饭了或者要邀请人吃饭,就用左手做个碗的样子,再用右手的食指和中指做筷子状,划向嘴的方向,像用筷子吃饭一样。
- 握手:现在,中国人见面握手很普遍。男人跟男人的握手会比较紧,也会上下摆动数次,以表中肯。但是男人跟女人的握手就很轻,或者只碰一下,或者只碰手指尖，怕显得亲近。
- "我"：用食指指自己的鼻子。
- 不行、不好、不对、不：摇头。
- 轻蔑：如果要表示轻视谁或什么事，就伸出小拇指，往上指。伸出小拇指，也示意人或事或东西微不足道。
- 羞：用食指尖不断斜着在脸上上下刮动。
- 羞辱：挨骂、受辱或失败的时候常会把头低下去，以示丢脸和见不得人。
- 请肃静：如果不让别人说话或者要别人安静一点，就会将食指向上伸，放在嘴前，但不碰到嘴。
- 微笑：微笑表示友善、了解或同意，但一般不对陌生人微笑。有时微笑也表示鼓励和同情。有时会看到有人向中国人诉说悲哀的事情时，对方会好像在微笑。这是因为对方不知说什么才好，只好以微笑表示同情。
- 惊讶：如果吃惊或吓一跳，人们会自然把嘴张大。
- 感谢：点头或鞠躬是表达感谢的动作。有时有人也会向前拉着对方的手握着摇几下。
- 好、同意：大拇指朝上。
- 不确定或尴尬：不知如何是好或者尴尬的时候，人们会嗤笑或小笑。
- 胜利手势：用食指和中指作"V"字形，手掌向外。如果在数数，这个形象就是"二"。如果两指做如剪的动作，就表示剪刀。
- "喂，你好"和"再见"：手臂伸出，手心朝外，手掌上下摇动。另一动作是手掌向上、向外，手指上下摆动。
- 好、对、同意：点头。

不礼貌的举止

对加拿大人和美国人来说：

- 夸大（除非很明显是在开玩笑）。
- 在人面前打嗝。
- 对着人咳嗽。
- 走着路吃东西。
- 在公共场合指点人。
- 在公共场所吐痰。
- 盯着陌生人看。
- 大声说话，特别是在公共场合大声说话。
- 在人面前打哈欠。

对中国人来说：

- 在饭馆请客时，当着客人的面付账。
- 用食指指人。
- 自己先给自己注满酒杯或茶杯，而没先给客人注满。
- 把脚放在桌子上，或者说话时坐在桌子上。
- 主人还没让座，自己就先坐下来。
- 说话时眼光不停地注视着人。
- 吃饭时，玩筷子或用筷子指人或指东西。

谚语的智慧

Proverbial expressions are distillations of widely accepted "pearls of wisdom" circulated and handed down from generation to generation. It is interesting and important to find out and to know that there are similar or even identical proverbial expressions in North American culture and Chinese culture because it shows that basically these two cultures have more in common than meets the eye. Even though they may be expressed somewhat differently, these apparently different ways may simply serve the same purpose, just as different expressions are used to express the same wisdom. Therefore, as we can also see from the following list of parallel proverbs, there are indeed different ways of expressing the same cultural values, so different paths may lead to the same goal.

谚语和成语是智慧的结晶，是一代一代传下来的。这是公认的事实。了解在北美和中国有同样或相似的说法很有意思，也很重要，因为我们从中就知道这两种文化，事实上有很多相同的地方。虽然它们的述说方式多少不一样，但是这些不同的述说方式还是为了达到相同的目标，即不同的说法表达同样的智慧。下列中英文对照的谚语和成语便表现出两方有很多同样或同等的说法和文化结晶，因之，这两种文化可以说是殊途同归的。

English Proverbial Expressions	中文谚语和成语
A baker's wife may bite of a bun, a brewer's wife may bite of a tun.	近水楼台先得月
A bad conscience is a snake in one's heart.	做贼心虚

A bad penny always comes back.	恶有恶报
A bad workman quarrels with his tools.	劣工嫌器
A bird in the hand is worth two in the bush.	多得不如现得
A black plum is as sweet as a white.	白猫黑猫，抓到老鼠就是好猫
Accidents will happen.	天有不测风云
Actions speak louder than words.	坐而言不如起而行
A clear conscience is a soft pillow.	白天不做亏心事，夜半敲门心不惊
A closed mouth catches no flies.	病从口入，祸从口出
A contented mind is perpetual feast.	知足常乐
Adversity makes strange bedfellows.	身处逆境不择友
A fall into the pit, a gain in your wit.	经一事，长一智
A friend in need is a friend indeed.	患难见真情
After meat, mustard.	雨后送伞
A good appetite is the best sauce.	饥不择食
A heavy snow promises a good harvest.	瑞雪兆丰年
A honey tongue, a heart of gall.	口蜜腹剑 / 笑里藏刀 / 佛口蛇心
A Jack of all trades and master of none.	万事皆通，一无所长
A little is better than none.	聊胜于无
A little leak will sink a great ship.	千丈之堤，溃于蚁穴
A little learning is a dangerous thing.	浅学误人
A little spark kindles a great fire.	星星之火，可以燎原
All good things came to an end.	天下无不散之宴席
All his geese are swans.	老王卖瓜，自卖自夸
All rivers run into the sea.	百川入海
All roads lead to Rome.	处处有路到长安
A man gets to know his companion on a long journey and in a little inn.	路遥知马力，日久见人心
A miss is as good as a mile.	失之毫厘，差之千里
A Monday morning quarterback.	事后诸葛亮

Among the blind the one-eyed man is king.	山中无老虎，猴子称霸王
An enemy's mouth seldom speaks well.	狗嘴里吐不出象牙来
An uncut gem goes not sparkle.	玉不琢，不成器
A word spoken is an arrow let fly.	一言既出，驷马难追
A stitch in time saves nine.	小洞不补，大洞吃苦
A straw shows which way the wind blows.	一叶便知秋
As you make your bed so you must lie on it.	自食其果
As wet as a drowned rat.	湿得像落汤鸡
Bad news travels fast.	好事不出门，坏事传千里
Beauty is in the eye of the beholder. / Beauty lies in lovers' eyes.	情人眼里出西施
Beggars can't be choosers.	饥不择食
Better an open enemy than a false friend.	明枪易躲，暗箭难防
Better a small fish than an empty dish.	有胜于无
Better be the head of an ass than the tail of a horse.	宁为鸡头，不为凤尾
Better the devil you know than the devil you don't.	明枪易躲，暗箭难防
Better to sail slowly than not to sail at all.	不怕慢，就怕站
Birds of a feather flock together.	物以类聚
Bite off more than one can chew.	贪多嚼不烂
Bite the hand that feeds one.	恩将仇报
By others' faults, wise men correct their own.	他山之石，可以攻玉
Cast pearls before swine.	对牛弹琴
Caught between the devil and the deep blue sea.	进退维谷/进退两难
Clothes make the man.	人靠衣裳，马靠鞍装
Clothes do not make the man.	人不可以貌相
Comparisons are odious.	人比人，气死人

Constant dripping wears away the stone.	滴水穿石
Courtesy costs nothing.	礼多人不怪
Covet all, lose all.	贪多必失
Cut the coat according to the cloth.	量布裁衣
Deep rivers move in silence, shallow brooks are noisy.	深水静静流，浅溪潺潺流
Despair gives courage to a coward.	人急造反，狗急跳墙
Diamond cut diamond.	强中更有强中手
Diet cures more than the doctor.	药补不如食补
Discretion is the better part of valour.	小心即大勇
Diseases come on horseback, but go away on foot.	病来如山倒，病去如抽丝
Do as you would be done by.	推己及人 / 己所不欲，勿施于人
Don't count your chickens before they are hatched.	勿打如意算盘
Don't cross the bridge until you come to it.	船到桥头自然直
Don't judge a book by its cover.	勿以貌取人 / 人不可貌相
Don't let the grass grow under your feet.	不失时机
Don't put all your eggs in one basket.	不要孤注一掷
Don't put off till tomorrow what should be done today.	今日事，今日毕
Don't wash your dirty linen in public.	家丑不可外扬
Do unto others as you would be done unto.	己所不欲，勿施于人
Drunkenness reveals what soberness conceals.	酒后吐真言
Easier said than done.	说话容易做事难
Easy as pie.	易如反掌
Easy come, easy go.	易得易失
Eat one's cake and have it too.	又要马儿好，又要马儿不吃草
Empty vessels make the most sound.	一瓶子不响，半瓶子晃荡

Even Homer sometimes nods.	人非圣贤，孰能无过 / 智者千虑，必有一失
Even the dog swaggers when its master wins favour.	狗仗人势 / 一人得道，鸡犬升天
Every advantage has its disadvantage.	有利必有弊
Every cook praises his own broth.	王婆卖瓜，自卖自夸
Every dog has his day.	十年河东，十年河西
Every man has his faults.	人孰无过 / 人无完人
Everyone to his taste.	人各有所好
Every potter praises his own pot./Every salesman boasts of his own wares.	老王卖瓜，自卖自夸
Fair face, foul heart.	人面兽心
Fame has its price.	人怕出名猪怕肥
Familiarity breeds contempt.	近庙欺神
First come first served.	捷足先登
Fish begins to stink at the head.	上梁不正下梁歪
Fishing in the air.	水中捞月
Forgive and forget.	不念旧恶
Fortune favours fools.	傻子有傻福
Fortune is fickle.	天有不测风云，人有旦夕祸福
Gather ye rosebuds while ye may.	有花堪折直须折
Gild the lily.	画蛇添足
Give him an inch and he'll take a yard/mile.	得寸进尺
God's mill grinds slow but sure.	天网恢恢，疏而不漏
Good medicine tastes bitter.	良药苦口，忠言逆耳
Greatest genius often lies concealed.	大智若愚

Habit is second nature.	习惯成自然
Half a loaf is better than none.	聊胜于无
Hardships never come alone.	祸不单行
Haste makes waste.	欲速则不达
He cries wine and sells vinegar.	挂羊头卖狗肉
He has a tiger by the tail.	骑虎难下
He is lifeless that is faultless.	人孰无过
He is rich enough who owes nothing.	无债就是富
He that sups with the devil must have a long spoon.	敬鬼神而远之
He that lies down with dogs must rise up with fleas./He that touches pitch will be defiled.	近墨者黑
He that will thrive must rise at five.	五更起床，百事兴旺
He who does not gain loses.	无所得即有所失
He who has a mind to beat his dog will easily find his stick.	欲加之罪，何患无辞
He who hesitates is lost.	举棋不定，坐失良机
He who risks nothing, gains nothing.	不入虎穴，焉得虎子
He who would catch fish must not mind getting wet.	欲擒龙王，就得下海
His bark is worse than his bite.	嘴硬心软 / 雷大雨小
Hunger finds no fault with the cookery.	饥不择食
If there were no clouds, we should not enjoy the sun.	吃得苦中苦，方知甜中甜
If we cannot get what we like, we have to like what we can get.	随遇而安
If you agree to carry the calf, they'll make you carry the cow.	得寸进尺
If you cannot bite, never show your teeth.	不能打仗，切莫出兵

If you have no hand, you cannot make a fist.	巧妇难为无米之炊
If you run after two hares, you will catch neither.	两头落空
If you sell the cow, you sell her milk too.	蚀了本也输了利 / 赔上夫人又折兵
If you want something done right, do it yourself.	求人不如求自己
Ill gotten, ill spent.	悖入悖出
In for a penny, in for a pound	一不做，二不休
In the end things will mend.	船到桥头自然直
In wine there is truth.	酒后吐真言
It is a small flock that has not a black sheep.	家家有本难念的经
It is never too late to learn.	活到老，学到老
It is no use crying over spilt milk.	泼水难收
It never rains, but it pours.	祸不单行
Kill the goose that laid the golden egg.	杀鸡取卵
Knowledge is power.	知识就是力量
Learn to walk before you run.	循序渐进
Leopards cannot change their spots.	江山易改，本性难移
Let bygones be bygones.	既往不咎
Let sleeping dogs lie.	别自找麻烦
Let things take their course.	听其自然
Life has its ups and downs.	十年河东，十年河西
Like a cat on a hot tin roof	热锅上的蚂蚁
Like a duck to water.	如鱼得水
Like attracts like.	物以类聚，人以群分
Like begets like./Like father, like son.	有其父必有其子
Like cures like.	以毒攻毒
Little strokes fell great oaks.	水滴石穿
Little things amuse little minds.	小人志卑

Live and learn.	活到老，学到老
Look before you leap.	三思而后行
Love is blind.	情人眼里出西施
Love me, love my dog.	爱屋及乌
Make haste slowly.	从容赶急
Make hay while the sun shines.	未雨绸缪 / 趁热打铁
Man proposes, God disposes.	谋事在人，成事在天
Many hands make light work.	众擎易举 / 众人拾柴火焰高
Measure another's corn by one's own bushel.	以己度人
Misery loves company.	同病相怜 / 祸不单行
Misfortunes never come alone.	祸不单行
Money makes the world go' round. /Money talks.	有钱能使鬼推磨
More apparent than real.	虚有其表
More haste, less speed.	欲速则不达
Much care brings grey hair.	忧虑催人老
Necessity is the mother of invention.	穷则变，变则通
Never cackle till your egg is laid.	事竟成，才声张
New brooms sweep clean.	新官上任三把火
Nobody is perfect.	人无完人
No garden without its weeds.	有利必有弊
No man is a hero to his valet.	近庙欺神
No pains, no gains./ No song, no supper./No sweat, no sweet.	不劳则无获
Nothing comes from nothing.	无风不起浪
Nothing ventured, nothing gained.	不入虎穴，焉得虎子
On the horns of a dilemma.	进退维谷 / 进退两难
One good turn deserves another.	善有善报

Out of debt, out of danger. 无债一身轻
Out of sight, out of mind. 眼不见，心不烦

People who live in glass houses should not throw stones. 正人先正己
Practice makes perfect. 熟能生巧
Pride comes before a fall. 骄者必败
Putting the horse before the cart. 本末倒置

Seeing is believing. 百闻不如一见
Six of one, half dozen of the other. 半斤八两
Speak of the devil and he is sure to appear. 说曹操曹操就到
Spectators see more than players. 旁观者清
Spend money like water. 挥金如土
Still water runs deep. 大智若愚 / 深藏不露

Take things as they come. 既来之，则安之
Tall trees catch much wind. 树大招风
Teaching grandmother to suck eggs. 班门弄斧
The bait hides the hook. 笑里藏刀
The calm after a storm 否极泰来
The coat makes the man. 佛要金装，人要衣装
The pot calls the kettle black. 五十步笑百步
There are two sides to every story. 公说公有理，婆说婆有理
There's no place like home. 金屋银屋比不上自己草屋
The walls have ears. 隔墙有耳
Throw out a sprat to catch a mackerel. 吃小亏占大便宜 / 抛砖引玉
Time and tide wait for no man. 岁月不等人
Time is money. 寸金难买寸光阴

To fish in troubled waters.	浑水摸鱼
Too many cooks spoil the broth.	七手八脚必败事
Two heads are better than one.	三个臭皮匠，顶个诸葛亮
We reap what we sow.	种瓜得瓜，种豆得豆
What can you expect from a pig but a grunt?	狗嘴里吐不出象牙来
What goes around comes around.	善有善报，恶有恶报
What's done cannot be undone.	木已成舟
When in Rome, do as the Romans do.	入乡要随俗
When the cat's away, the mice will play.	阎王不在，小鬼作怪
Where there is smoke there is fire.	无风不起浪
Where there is a will, there is a way.	有志者，事竟成
While there is life, there is hope.	留得青山在，不怕没柴烧
Words cut more than swords.	舌剑利于刀剑
You can't run with the hare and hunt with the hounds.	两面讨好
You can't teach an old dog new tricks.	老狗熊学不会新玩意儿
You get what you pay for.	一分钱，一分货
You must lie in the bed you have made.	自作自受
You can't make a silk purse out of a sow's ear.	狗嘴里吐不出象牙

根据以上各项，我们知道北美和中国文化有同有异。然而，不同并非对错，而只是"殊途同归"罢了。

CROSS-CULTURAL PERSPECTIVES: NORTH AMERICA AND CHINA

Yvonne Li Walls and Jan W. Walls

（［加］李盈　王健　著）

About the Authors

Yvonne Li Walls (李盈) received her master degree from the University of Washington in Comparative Literature and completed her Ph.D. program in Comparative Literature in Indiana University. In the United States, she taught at the University of Washington, Indiana University and University of Minnesota. She also taught at the Taiwan Normal University, Taiwan University; Aichi University in Japan; and the University of British Columbia, the University of Victoria, the Lester B. Pearson College of the Pacific and Simon Fraser University in Canada. She has published many works in Chinese and English translation.

Jan W. Walls (王健) received his master and Ph.D. degrees from Indiana University in Chinese language and literature. He taught at Indiana University, Aichi University in Japan, and the University of British Columbia, the University of Victoria and Simon Fraser University in Canada. He has published many English translations of Chinese poetry and literature.

Yvonne and Jan have co-authored and co-translated the following publications: English translations of Chinese poems by Zheng Banqiao and Wang Kaiyun in *Waiting for the Unicorn; Zhìguànxiàng* (Chinese translation of *Cannery Row*); *100 Allegorical Tales From Traditional China* (English translation of *Yùyán gùshì bǎizé*); *West Lake: A Collection of Folktales* (English translation of *Xīhú mínjiān gùshì*); English translations in *Paintings by Chinese Masters* (60 volumes); *Classical Chinese Myths*; and *Using Chinese*.

Preface

During our nearly four decades of teaching Chinese language and cross-cultural communication to North American university students, they frequently asked us: "Why do they say it this way?" or "What is the logic behind this pattern of behavior?" To answer such questions, we could have simply replied: "Because 1.3 billion Chinese think it makes sense this way," but we chose rather to demonstrate how English and Chinese language and thought patterns are mostly different ways of seeing and expressing the same situations. The same is true of differences in cultural values and their modes of expression. They are, as we remind the reader several times in this book, "different paths to the same goal."

Any social situation may be anticipated, seen, described and interpreted from many different angles, depending on how the situation fits into the worldview of the viewer. For example, an American or Canadian visiting Chinese friends might bring a box of chocolates as a gift, and wonder why the Chinese host doesn't even open the box to appreciate the gift; conversely, a Chinese person visiting North American friends might also bring a box of chocolates as a gift, and be somewhat surprised when the host opens the box and then offers the chocolates for everyone to enjoy. The North American might not know that Chinese often do not open gifts right away, especially if there are other guests present, so as not to embarrass anyone through comparison; and the Chinese might not know that in the West, the host is expected to show appreciation for the gift in front of everyone.

This book is written in two languages — English and Chinese. Both texts address the same topics and sub-topics. We begin by looking at the differences in modes of expression for everyday concepts, such as addresses, dates, time, names and ways of addressing people. From these differences we can see right away that, different as they may be, each conveys the same information required by the situation, and there is simply no question of whether one way is right and the other wrong, they are indeed simply different paths to the same goal. We discuss the cultural logic of differences in conceiving, organizing and expressing everyday events, such as dining and seating customs, gift giving, greetings and farewells, thanks and apologies. We see and discuss interesting commonalities and differences in North American and Chinese symbolic values attached to colours, numbers, animals and birds, flowers and plants, so that people may understand each other better. We continue to explore differences in non-verbal behaviour, whose significance most of us simply take for granted — eye contact, touching, synchronization, silence, gestures, etc.

We conclude with a most enlightening comparison of North American English and Chinese proverbial wisdom, illustrating how fundamentally similar traditional wisdom may be expressed through quite different metaphors. This is perhaps the most compelling argument to support the idea that differences on the surface are not fundamental differences, since different cultures are after all just "different paths to the same goal."

Yvonne Li Walls and Jan W. Walls in Vancouver, Canada

Table of Contents

Preamble ·· 59

Social Communication ·························· 64

Address, Date and Time ························ 64

Names and Forms of Address ···················· 67

Business Cards ································ 69

Individual, Group and Family ···················· 69

Personal Relationship ·························· 71

Explicitness and Implicitness ···················· 72

Dining and Seating ···························· 72

Gift-Giving ···································· 74

Greetings and Farewells ························ 75

Attitude towards Age ·························· 76

Thanks and Apologies·························· 77

CROSS-CULTURAL PERSPECTIVES: NORTH AMERICA AND CHINA

Symbolism ······78
- Colours ······78
- Numbers ······82
- Animals and Birds ······87
- Flowers and Plants ······92

Non-verbal Behaviour and Body Language ······96
- Non-verbal Behaviour ······96
- Gestures and Body Language ······101
- Impolite Behaviour ······108

Proverbial Wisdom ······110

Preamble

In the Western world there are sayings like:

Heaven is a place where

- The police are British.
- The chefs are French.
- The lovers are Italian.
- And everything is organized by the Germans.

And,

Hell is a place where

- The police are French.
- The chefs are British.
- The lovers are German.
- And everything is organized by the Italians.

It has been said that among East Asians:

The best life comes from having

- A Japanese wife.
- A Chinese chef.
- An American house.

And,

The worst life comes from having

- A Chinese house.
- A Japanese chef.
- An American wife.

The above sayings are humorous to most people because they play upon simplistic and stereotypic generalizations. Viewed positively, they point out some commonly observed and believed characteristics of people from different nations and cultures. But we should always bear in mind that the French are much more than good chefs and Italians much more than good lovers; and not all Japanese wives are submissive, nor all Chinese houses cramped by Western standards.

Thus there are both opportunities and pitfalls in comparing cultures. In taking a comparative approach to the study of cultures, we should bear in mind that we can only use the more widely observed features which may not apply to all of the people of the national cultures compared. Thus, in order to avoid the mistaken view that "They (the people of a certain country) are all the same," we must make an effort to understand the people better and their cultures more deeply.

There are culturally conditioned differences between peoples, but differences do not automatically imply right or wrong. Although difference may be a source of chaos, it is also the source of energy and the source of dynamism. Differences should be celebrated rather than regarded as objects of ridicule or obstacles to understanding.

Consider water: without a difference in levels, water will stand still and become stagnant. It is only with difference that water can flow.

Joseph Campbell (1904 — 1987) says it well:

> "The separateness apparent in the world is secondary. Beyond that world of opposites is an unseen, but experienced unity and identity in us all." (*The Hero with a Thousand Faces. By Joseph Campbell.* London: Fontana-Harper, 1993, p. 162.)

There are apparent differences between cultures, but we must also bear in mind that as human beings we are essentially very similar. Chinese people have known this for many centuries, and the first line of the first primer all educated Chinese used to memorize says: "At the beginning of life, people are basically good. They are fundamentally similar, but drawn apart by different experiences." (*Three-Character Classic, Sān Zì Jīng*)

Fig.1 Different Is Not Wrong; It Is just Different
by Yvonne Walls

Life and human interaction would be easier to understand if we could make everybody the same again, would it not? But since it is neither possible nor desirable that everybody and all cultures be made the same, and since it is desirable to keep a certain difference between cultures so that our world can be more colorful and beautiful, we need to understand different cultures and the meaning of cultural difference. Through making comparisons we can understand different people better and thus reduce intercultural conflicts and cross-cultural misunderstandings.

Comparing Canada, U.S.A. and China

Table 1   Comparision of Canada, U.S.A. and China

Country	Canada	U.S.A.	China
Area	9,984,670 sq km (world's second largest country, after Russia)	9,826,675 sq km (world's third largest country)	9,596,961 sq km (world's fourth largest country, after Russia, Canada and the U.S.)
Population	34,568,211 (world's no. 37)	316,668,567 (world's no. 3)	1,349,585,838 (world's no. 1)
Density	3.5 per sq km	32 per sq km	137 per sq km
Bordering Countries	U.S.A.	Canada, Mexico	Afghanistan, Bhutan, Burma, India, Kazakhstan, North Korea, Kyrgyzstan, Laos, Mongolia, Nepal, Pakistan, Russia (northeast), Russia (northwest), Tajikistan, Vietnam
Ethnic Groups	British Isles origin 28%; French origin 23%; Other European 15%; First nations 2%; other 6%; mixed background 26%	White 79.96%, Black 12.85%, Asian 4.43%, Native 0.97%, other	Han Chinese, 91.5%; 55 other minority nationalities, 8.5%
Official Languages	English 58.8% and French 21.6%, etc.	English (most speakers)	Pǔtōnghuà (Mandarin)
Urban Population	71%	82%	47%

By looking at the above comparisons (see Table 1), we can see that the physical and socio-cultural situation of China is much more complex than that of Canada and the U.S., especially considering the size of population and number of neighboring countries. On the other hand, Canada has immigrants from more than 200 and the U.S. has immigrants from more than 80 different country origins, while immigrants are very few in China by comparison.

Canada has one neighboring country and five and a half time zones, the U.S. has two neighboring countries and four time zones, while China has 14 neighboring countries, and only one time zone. This would indicate that, at least, the concept of time has a more local and dispersed focus in Canada and the U.S. but is more centralized and unified in China. This concept of diversity versus uniformity in time zones may be revealed in other cultural aspects as well.

Cross-cultural Communication Study Premise

• There are more similarities than differences.

• Difference is often over-emphasized.

• Cultures function as different paths to similar goals.

Purpose of Cross-cultural Communication Study

To Understand a Different Culture in Order to Reduce Cross-Cultural Misunderstanding and the Potential for Conflict.

A Summary Comparison of North American and Chinese Cultural Characteristics

Table 2   Comparison of North American and Chinese Cultural Characteristics

North Americans	Chinese
Stress independence	Stress interdependence
Individual is seen as very important	Individual is seen as part of group
Understanding oneself is seen as most important	Interpersonal harmony is more important
Equality is seen as important	Hierarchy is accepted as necessary
Arguments are seen as paths to truth	Open argument is seen as divergence
Success is seen as personal achievement	Success is attributed to group effort
Privacy is seen as rather important	Privacy is seen as less important

Social Communication

Address, Date and Time

Language is a communication medium that also expresses culture. An English saying goes: "Take care of the dimes and the dollars will take care themselves." This, in a sense, indicates that many things are conceived, expressed and acted upon from smaller to larger units in English speaking countries like Canada and the United States. However, a Chinese saying goes: "大处着眼，小处着手，dàchù zhuóyǎn, xiǎochù zhúoshǒu (keep your eyes on the whole while dealing with the parts)." This would indicate that Chinese tend to maintain a focus on larger pictures while dealing with smaller details or components.

Here are some examples:

Address

When writing an address on an envelope in English the order, written horizontally, is as follows:
- Name of recipient
- Number of residence + Street
- City + Province
- Country

Example: Mr. John Smith

4444 Walnut Street

Vancouver, B.C.

Canada

When writing an address on an envelope in Chinese the order, written horizontally, is as follows:

- Country
- Province + City
- Street + Number of residence
- Name of recipient

Example: Zhōngguó   (China

          Shāndōng, Jǐnán   Shandong Province, Jinan

          Gǔtíng Street, 8888 hào   Guting Street, No. 8888

          Wú Círén Xiānsheng shōu   Wu Ciren Mr., Receive)

Date

When a complete date is expressed in English, the order is generally:

- Day of the week
- Day of the month
- Month
- Year
- A certain day

Example: It was Friday, the 28th of December, 2012 that day.

Or

- A certain day
- Day of the week
- Month
- Day
- Year

Example: That day was Friday, December 28, 2012.

When a date is expressed in Chinese, the order is:

- A certain day
- Year
- Month
- Day
- Day of the week

Example: Nàtiān shì 2012 nián, shí'èr yuè, èrshíbā rì, xīngqī wǔ.

(That day was 2012 year, twelfth month, twenty-eighth day, weekday five.)

Time

In English:
- Minute
- Second (past)
- O'clock

Example: It is now 3 minutes and 20 seconds past 5 o'clock.

In Chinese:
- O'clock
- Minute
- Second

Example: Xiànzài wǔdiǎn sānfēn èrshí miǎo.

(It is now 5 o'clock, 3 minutes and 20 seconds.)

From the above examples, we can see that almost all the ways of conceiving and expressing address, date and time in English are in a pyramid form where the individual or the smaller units are on the bottom and move upward. On the other hand, the ways of telling address, date and time in Chinese are in an inverted pyramid form where the individual and the smaller units are at the top. This parallels the fact that in North American cultures, the individual is regarded as primary, while in Chinese culture, the individual is regarded as secondary, always expressed as an element of a greater unit such as family, clan or society.

In summary we can see that the North American way of expressing the above is like a pyramid, while the Chinese way is like an upside down pyramid.

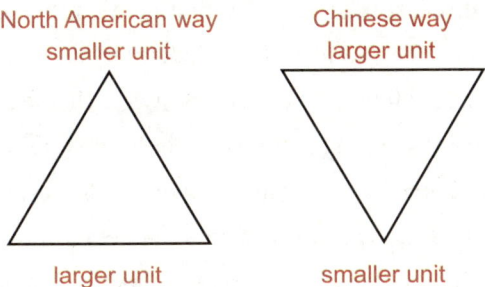

Fig. 2　Comparison of North American and Chinese Ways of Conceiving and Expressing Address, Date and Time

Names and Forms of Address

In North America, a full name consists of the first name, a middle name and the last name, although some people may not have middle names. The order is: first name + middle name + last name (surname). For example: Mary Allen Smith. In non-formal situations, when a person is introduced or introduces himself/herself, the first name is often used. The first name is also often used during introduction to show friendliness. When a woman is married, she normally adopts her husband's last name, either dropping her own maiden last name or adding her husband's last name at the end. In the case of Mary Allen Smith, she can become Mary Allen Smith Jones or Mary Allen Jones or Mary Smith Jones; and she will be referred to as Mrs. Jones. A son often can have the same given name as the father and be known as junior. For example, John Barrie Jones's son might be named John Barrie Jones, Jr. However, a daughter cannot be named junior with her mother's first name or her father's first name. When addressing an individual, the form is: title of address + last name, for example: President Jones, Dr. Smith, Professor Wilson, etc. However, titles such as director, manager, teacher, worker, etc. are not used for addressing the person. In such cases, one uses Mr., Mrs., Ms., or Miss.

In China, people of minority nationalities such as the Miao, the Mongolians or the

Tibetans, may have multi-syllable names. In the case of the majority Han Chinese, a full name consists of the last name and the first name, in the order of: family name (surname) + given name. The family name is usually one character (one syllable) and the given name can be either two characters (two syllables) or one character (one syllable). In Chinese, there is no equivalent to the English middle name. There are a small number of family names that consist of two characters, so the longest possible Han Chinese name can be four characters (four syllables). In the case of two-character given names, the first character may be a generation name, that is, all the sons and male cousins of the same generation will share one character in their given names. This can also be the case with female names, but not as often as with males. It indicates that traditionally males have been viewed as more important than females because it is they who retain the family name and carry on the family lineage. However, a son cannot be named after his father, as that would be considered most disrespectful. On the other hand, given names do not have to contain a generation name. There are no set first names in Chinese. Generally speaking, first names usually contain good meanings. For example, a male's name may be: Yīngxióng (hero) or Zhìwěi (great ambition); and a female's name may be: Yǎxiù (elegant and beautiful) or Ruòlán (like orchard), etc. Traditionally, when a woman was married, she would either drop her own surname and use her husband's surname or precede her own full name with her husband's surname. In modern times, a woman does not have to take on her husband's family name after

Fig. 3 "This Is Director Wang; This Is Manager Li. This Is Our President, John" by Yvonne Walls

she is married. She most often continues to be known by her maiden name. When addressing a person, the most polite way is: surname + title, for example: Li President, Wang Professor, Liu Doctor, Zhang Teacher, Qian Worker, etc. Anyone who has a title should be addressed with it. If not, the addresses can be Wang Mister, Wang Mrs., or Wang Miss.

Business Cards

North Americans, particularly business people or people with some status, do exchange business cards, but the way of exchanging business cards is comparatively more casual than most Chinese would expect. The card is simply handed over to the other person, normally using only one hand.

Business cards traditionally were not used by Chinese until China was opened up to the West. Nowadays, business people and government officials exchange business cards when first introduced. The most polite way of exchanging business cards is to hand over one's own card with both hands and receive the other person's card also with both hands as a sign of respect. Ideally, one should show interest in the other person by reading the card attentively before putting it away. If there are two or more new business acquaintances seated at a meeting table, the business cards may be placed on the table in the same order as the new acquaintances are seated, making it easier to connect new names to faces.

Individual, Group and Family

In English the written word "I" is capitalized no matter where it appears and it may never be omitted, even when clearly understood as the subject, whereas "you" and other pronouns are capitalized only when they begin a sentence. This is an indication of how important "I" (also referred to as "the first person") is perceived relative to "you," "he," "she" and "it."

The capitalization of "I" may also be emblematic of the fact that the individual is regarded as the fundamental unit of North American society. The "privacy" of the individual is also a very important notion that must be respected; the same is true of independence. Individualists do not want to appear to be like everyone else. For example, people may wish to show that they are in tune with the latest fashion trends and colours, but at the same time their particular combination should appear to be uniquely their own. Children are encouraged to be independent from early in life: They learn to eat and to wash and do other things on their own as soon as they can. To be independent is to be admired and emulated. During vacation times, people like to go to places "far from the madding crowd" and to be as alone as possible. Because of the importance of this sense of individuality and independence, Canadian and American societies are rather egalitarian, which may help explain why their authority figures can be criticized and even ridiculed to an extent that would surprise most Chinese observers. This is because ordinary people are the ones who, through the electoral process, delegate political authority to their elected officials. In Canada and the U.S. we frequently see satirical cartoons, stand-up comic monologues and skits that ridicule or make fun of political figures at all levels of government.

In the Chinese language, the character for "wǒ" ("I", "me") is written the same whether it is the subject of a sentence or the object of a verb. As well, once "wǒ" is established as the topic, it can be omitted both in writing and in conversation. For centuries the concept of individual privacy has been almost non-existent for the majority of Chinese. It is recently becoming a concept for some, but the Chinese word for "privacy" is a translated concept rendered as "yǐnsī (hide personal; hide selfish)" which actually may convey negative connotations that are not present at all in the English word. Interdependence traditionally has been far more important in Chinese culture than independence. Children are helped to eat, to wash and to dress for a much longer time than a North American would imagine. The "group spirit" (tuántǐ jīngshén) is also praised as more important than individuality in Chinese culture. During vacation time, people like to go join the crowd rather than run away from it. The Chinese word "rènào" is difficult to translate into a very positive concept in English, because it means a lot of hustle and bustle and a lot of noise and a lot of people. Chinese society is not as egalitarian as North American societies. Individual authority figures are supposed to be respected and not criticized, much less publicly ridiculed. Children are expected to respect, obey and listen to their elders and parents. Recently, because of the one-child policy, people worry about a whole generation of children being so spoiled that they will not behave well. We have seen a Chinese cartoon that satirizes a child who directs his parents with an orchestra conductor's baton in hand, simultaneously ridiculing the parents who actually tolerate such a behavior.

Personal Relationship

Personal relationship is not considered the most important factor in North American society although everyone would agree that it often helps. When seeking employment or doing business, a North American does not like to appear to have to rely upon personal relationship, because what is important is one's own ability. Friendship is not necessarily expected to last forever; it may last as long as there is mutual interest, or mutual benefit involved. To have graduated from the same school does not necessarily make a schoolmate your friend. Colleagues are simply people who happen to work together, so they may be friendly and cooperative in the workplace, but they do not necessarily consider each other to be friend. By the time of senior high school and university, teachers and students often talk to each other as equals and they may even be "on a first name basis." Again, the teacher-student relationship is not expected to be long lasting after graduation.

In a Chinese situation, however, personal relationships or "guānxì (connections)" are traditionally regarded as very important in society. Having connections or not having connections may make a difference in what kind of job you will secure, what schools your children can gain admission to, or whether a business deal can be made or carried out smoothly or not. Friendship between Chinese, ideally at least, should be long lasting. Schoolmates and colleagues at work will almost necessarily become friends — this is one way connections are formed. Students are always supposed to show respect towards their teachers (whether they truly respect them or not), and a teacher-student relationship is generally expected to be long lasting after graduation.

Explicitness and Implicitness

In North America, one rule for communication is to "call a spade a spade" ("don't beat around the bush"), so people, especially in business negotiations, generally try to be clear and direct in their speech. They generally say what they mean and do not beat around the bush. Although "face" is respected, it is not a major consideration during interaction. Moreover, one does not normally try to "give face." Conflicts and arguments will happen, but they are not necessarily viewed as bad, because it is believed that they may even produce some unexpected improvements. And people's feelings are not necessarily hurt by such open conflicts.

In a Chinese society, the general communication rule is to be clear but not blunt. "Face" is very important in this regard. One not only should never make another person "lose face" in front of others, but also should try to "give face" to another person to make that person look good and feel good among his or her peers. In turn, this person will be expected to do you similar favours. Direct expression of conflicts and arguments is looked upon unfavorably because it may cause feelings to be hurt and "face" to be lost. Therefore, conflicting opinions are sometimes expressed indirectly, meaning that one has to look for meaning "between the lines." Conflicts are best settled privately, as during a recess or coffee break.

Dining and Seating

Formal dining in Canada and the U.S. generally takes place at an oblong table where the host and hostess sit at either end of the table. The chief male guest is seated to the right of the hostess and the chief female guest sits to the right of the host. The rest may

Fig. 4   Western Formal Table Setting   by Yvonne Walls

be seated in any order, but generally the ideal is to seat a male next to a female. Either the hostess or the host generally decides on who sits where, and the guests do not take seats until their positions are clear. Each person has his or her own set of dining ware and knives and forks, which are usually laid out on the table beforehand. White tablecloth and napkins are the norm and are generally used. It is a taboo to pick up any bowls or plates, or to make any noise when eating or drinking. In order to scoop up the remaining soup at the bottom of a bowl, one does not pick it up but rather tips the soup bowl forward away from one so that it will be easier to scoop up the remaining soup with a spoon. When food comes, it will be passed around and the guests are expected to "help themselves." In practical terms, this means that the guest is allowed to take as much or as little of each dish as she or he pleases, and is expected to eat all that is taken. When dining out with others, sometimes they may decide to "go Dutch," which means each pays for his/her own meal, by requesting separate cheques.

Formal Chinese dinners usually take place at a round table where the main host sits facing the door and the chief guest sits to his or her right and the second important guest to his or her left. The hostess sits across from him and sometimes the second important guest may sit to her right. There is a practical reason why the guest at a Chinese dinner sits to the right of the host: The polite host uses the "serving chopsticks" with the right hand to place food from the serving dish onto the guest's personal plate to

Fig. 5 Chinese Formal Table Setting
by Yvonne Walls

be polite. In some cases, when there are equal numbers of hosts and guests, they will be seated in such a way that a host will sit next to a guest to take care of the guest. Guests at a Chinese dinner do not have to be seated with a male next to a female. In fact, sometimes one side of the table may be males and the other side females, supposedly for convenience of conversation. Red or gold tablecloth and napkins are often used for formal occasions. The serving dishes will be put on a "lazy susan" so there is no need for picking up whole plates of food for serving. Small soup bowls and rice bowls can be picked up to mouth-level for easier drinking or eating. Some Chinese may even make a slurping noise when drinking soup, and this is not considered impolite, since the sucking in of air together with very hot soup can cool it down to a more comfortable level. In recent times, a guest can start to "serve himself" after being served a few dishes by the host to his left. For sanitary reasons, a pair of "serving chopsticks" and a "serving spoon" are to be used for serving the guests or oneself. When eating out with others, usually the one who suggests dining out will pay, although everyone may make a symbolic struggle for the bill when it is brought to the table. Those who do not get to pay this time will be expected to reciprocate another time. Generally Chinese people do not "go Dutch."

Gift-Giving

For North Americans, during formal official visits to China, gift exchanges usually are expected, and often the gifts may be larger coffee table books or albums of scenic spots of the visitor's country or province or city. The gifts may bear the logo of the government, the university or the company represented, or they may be representative arts and crafts from the visitor's country. In North America other occasions when gifts are usually given include presents for the hosts at home dinners, at birthdays, weddings and Christmas. If one is invited to a home dinner, one may bring flowers, a box of chocolates or a bottle of wine. For birthdays and Christmas, the gifts are usually more personal. For weddings, the gifts are ordinarily things the newlyweds can use to set up a new home: paintings, bed sheets, cookware, dinnerware, tablecloths, etc. Money is usually not given. Instead, one might give gift certificates so that the newlyweds can go and choose what they need. Aside from wedding presents, which are not opened until after the ceremony, most other presents may be opened right away.

In a Chinese situation, exchanging gifts is considered an important symbolic ritual and the gifts for formal official visits to Canada or the U.S. are similar to those that North Americans might give in a similar situation. Most of the time, Chinese will entertain in restaurants instead of at home. Gifts may be given to the host or hostess, and normally people reciprocate by inviting the host and hostess out for dinner later. During Chinese New Year, elders give red envelopes with money inside to children or unmarried young adults in their family. Older people's birthdays are celebrated with dinner parties. Gifts for newlyweds are usually in the form of money in red envelopes. Gifts to avoid are clocks, handkerchiefs, or green hats or caps for married men. "To wear a green hat or cap" means to be cuckolded. When giving a present in person, one should present it with both hands to show respect. Wrapped gifts are usually not opened in front of the presenter when gifts are exchanged, for fear of embarrassment (or "face loss") if there should be a large discrepancy in value between the two sides.

Greetings and Farewells

Greetings and farewells in Canada and the U.S. are friendly but more casual than a

Chinese person might expect. North Americans who are visited in their office or home do not usually go out of their way to formally welcome the guests beyond offering to hang up their coats and hats, nor would they feel obliged to walk a guest to the door or beyond the door when they leave, especially if there are other guests remaining in the room.

In a Chinese situation, however, ritual greetings and farewells are taken more seriously. People who are visited in offices usually walk with a departing guest to the door and beyond. Visitors to one's home may be accompanied not just to the door, but also all the way to the car or bus stop, or for quite a walking distance. In traditional China, this was seen as symbolizing a genuine reluctance to say goodbye. Now, it is a showing of good manners.

Attitude towards Age

In North America where so much emphasis is placed upon the ideal of dynamic youth, people, especially women, do not normally ask each other's age, which is considered personal. People generally do not feel the necessity of revealing their age to a new acquaintance, since there is little difference in discourse used between people with no dramatic difference in age. Actually it is considered impolite to ask a woman's age. In such a youth-oriented society, many older people are afraid of growing "useless" and therefore less respected. Thus older people often do not want to admit they are old, and feel proud of their relative independence. Once during an international conference, a Chinese delegate wanted to thank the representative of the organizers by saying, "Tā niánjì yǐjīng zhème dà le, … ," and the interpreter said, "And she is already so old… ." The whole audience burst out laughing. Another instance concerns a young Chinese who was standing in line just behind an older Western lady who was about to climb onto the bus when the young Chinese instinctively reached out to help her. She was incensed by this uninvited assistance, and shouted at him, "I'm NOT that old!"

In a Chinese situation, most people do not hesitate to offer their age voluntarily or to ask about another person's age. Often people in their forties will claim that they are getting old. It is only in recent years that younger urban women begin to be annoyed at being asked how old they are. Older people have accumulated a rich reservoir of experience and knowledge, so they are to be respected. They are to be helped whenever possible, and seats on public transit should be yielded to them. In the 1980's, Westerners riding on Chinese busses in Beijing were quite amused at reading the prominent sign that boasted: "This civilized bus offers seating priority to the elderly, the handicapped, the pregnant and the foreign." Children and young adults often address older people as: yéye (grandpa) or nǎinai (grandma) where North Americans would simply say "sir" or "ma'am." It is extremely rude simply to address an elderly Chinese as "old man" or "old woman."

Thanks and Apologies

Canadians are seen by Americans as a rather polite people. They say "Thank You!" and "Sorry!" very often, even to friends and family members. There is a joke about Canadians that says a Canadian even says "Sorry!" when someone accidently bumps into him. Canadians, it is widely believed, are quite humble. There is a joke about this too: Upon hearing a compliment, a Canadian always turns around and looks behind to see for whom it was intended.

Chinese people also say "Thank you!" and "I'm sorry." However, these words are not used in just any context. To use these expressions often to people you know very well or to your own family members would be to put some distance between yourself and those close to you. Therefore, sometimes appreciation is shown with facial expressions or by reciprocation. One significant difference in the way North Americans and Chinese use or do not use their "thank you" is in response to a flattering comment: a North American receiving a glowing comment on her dress or her hat, for example, would say "Why, thank you!" whereas a typical Chinese response might be a polite form of denial, like "nǎli, nǎli" ("Not at all").

Symbolism

Colours

Colours are not only beautiful in enriching human life, they are also used for practical purposes such as colour coding which is widely used around the world to communicate very specific and important information. Furthermore, different cultures associate different meanings with different colours to express feelings, such as joy, sadness, anger, jealousy or love. These differences reflect cultural traditions, and we may find great diversity in the use of colours and their associations between different cultures, and even within the same culture in different time periods. Such differences between Chinese and North American colour symbolism are often great, and though convergence is occurring, some of the differences are still significant.

In North American Culture:

- Black: Black is a colour of night and darkness that conceals the forces of evil and symbolizes death; but it is also a colour of power and sophistication. It is the colour of clothing worn at funerals, symbolizing both mourning and solemnity. Black is also worn for other very formal occasions, where a lady might wear a black evening gown, or the groom and the best man might wear black suits at a wedding, or men might wear black suits at a black-tie dinner. There are many expressions associated with black, such as: black comedy, black list, blackmail, black market, black sheep, and black Friday.

- Blue: Blue is the colour of a clear sky and calm seas and it symbolizes peace, calm, purity; but it may also be connected to feelings of sadness, depression and loneliness, as in "feeling blue." It is one of the most popular colours because people feel safe with this colour and it is generally the colour chosen for clothes to be worn by baby boys. These are popular expressions using blue: blue blood, blue film, true blue, once in a blue moon, and out of the blue.

- Green: Green is the colour of nature, symbolizing springtime, fertility, youth and hope; it is also associated with inexperience and jealousy. It is a colour attached to environmental friendliness as in "go green," and it is the colour that denotes safety, as in the use of green light. Other expressions connected with green are: give the green light, greenback, greenhorn, green thumb, green with envy, and turn green.

- Pink: Pink is symbolic of romance, pure love and gentleness. Since it is a colour of gentleness, it has the power to reduce aggression. It is generally a colour chosen for gift items given to baby girls. Pink-related expressions include: in the pink, pink slip and tickled pink.

- Red: Red is the colour of blood, so it symbolizes life and vitality. As a result, it represents strong feelings and energy. It is also the colour of fire, symbolizing destruction and danger. Red can easily attract attention, so it is associated with a "brazen" attitude. It is also a colour of danger, as can be seen in using the red light as a stop light for traffic. Red is used in these common phrases: caught red-handed, in the red, red alert, red carpet treatment, red in the face, red flag, red light district, red tape, red-letter day and seeing red.

- White: White is the colour of fresh snow and milk; it symbolizes purity and cleanliness, for example: a bride's wedding gown is traditionally white, white flowers are used in weddings, and doctors traditionally wear white coats. A home with a white picket fence represents a peaceful and happy home. White related expressions include: white Christmas, white elephant, white flag, white lie, and white terror.

- Yellow: Yellow is the colour of the sun, so it denotes optimism. It is also a colour that attracts attention. Taxicabs and school buses in North America are often colored yellow. It is a colour of caution, indicating that danger may be near, as in a "yellow alert." On a traffic light it means: "be careful" because the light is about to turn red. Informally, it is also used to symbolize cowardice, as in the derisive comment, "He's yellow," or "He is yellow-bellied." "Yellow journalism" means unscrupulously sensational journalistic reports.

In Chinese Culture:

- Black (hēisè): It is not a very good colour, as it signifies night, darkness and mourning. In recent years, black armbands are also used for mourning; a black ribbon is usually put at the top of the picture of the deceased at a funeral; and a black box is put around a printed name to indicate the person has passed away. Someone who is ruthless is said to be "black hearted, hēixīn." There are some black related words with negative connotations: "black hand gang, hēishǒudǎng" is the mafia; "hēishì" is the black market; "black speech, hēihuà" is secret words of the thieves; and a "black visitor, hēikè" is a hacker. Since colours are associated with directions, material and seasons, black is associated with the north, water and winter.

- Blue (lánsè): Considered an unlucky colour by some Chinese. "Blue bridge, lánqiáo," on the other hand, is a metaphor for the place where lovers meet.

- Gold (jīnsè): An auspicious colour symbolizing nobility, riches and honour. Chinese love gold and love to wear gold. It is closely related to ancient emperors. "To be listed on the gold list, jīnbǎng tímíng" means to have passed the civil examinations and having one's name listed on the list of successful examinees, one of the most important events in a man's life. "A house full of gold and jade, jīnyù mǎntáng" describes how rich a family is.

- Green (lǜsè): Green is the colour of nature and is a good colour in general; green jade represents beauty, good luck and virtue. In modern times, green has become the colour for a healthy clean environment, as in "to greenify, lǜhuà." "Green food, lǜsè shíwù" means food that is free of pesticides, and organic. However, to say that a married man "wears a green hat, dài lǜmàozi" means he has been cuckolded. Green is associated with the east, with spring and vegetation.

- Pink (fěnhóngsè): This is a colour that represents love now.

- Red (hóngsè): This is the most auspicious colour for the Chinese. It is the colour for good luck and auspicious occasions, such as weddings and Chinese New Year. The bride wears red and the groom will wear a red bow or sash. In big cities, brides now often wear a white wedding gown because of Western influence, but may wear pink or red shoes, or carry pink or red flowers. The bedroom of the newly-weds is decorated in red with red bedding. Red is definitely the most important colour during the Chinese New Year. Children wear red clothes for the New Year, and adults will wear something with red on it. Adults give children good luck money in red envelops. One sees red knots, red lanterns, red couplets, red paper cuttings, and red fire crackers everywhere. "Red-eye disease, hóngyǎnbìng" refers to jealousy. Red is associated with the south, with fire and the summer season.

- White (báisè): This is not an auspicious colour. It is the colour of death, mourning and ghosts. Off-white is the traditional colour of mourning, although currently "in mourning" is symbolized by wearing a black armband. Gifts should not be wrapped in white. "White speech, báishuō" means wasted words, wasted breath; "white jade without flaw, báiyù wúxiá" is used to describe perfect people and things. White is associated with the west, with metal and autumn.

- Yellow (huángsè): Yellow is an important colour for Chinese. This colour represents power and authority as well as earth. It was the colour for emperors who wore yellow robes and sat on a yellow throne. The Yellow Emperor is regarded as the founder of Chinese civilization. Yellow is also associated with things pornographic, such as "yellow movie, huángsè diànyǐng" referring to blue films, "yellow magazines, huángsè zázhì" indicating pornographic magazines, and "yellow springs, huángquán" refers to the netherworld. It is associated with earth and with the centre.

Numbers

Numbers take on different meanings in different cultures. Some numbers may be considered lucky, perhaps because of a traditional belief that certain numbers have "lucky energy," while other numbers may be considered unlucky because of some negative associations. Some people may believe in it while others may not. Some Chinese people will publicly deny belief in such "superstitions," but do not mind paying extra fees to obtain lucky numbers on their license plates, and some North Americans laugh at superstitions, but would feel uncomfortable with "666" on their license plate.

In North American Culture:

- "3" plays a very important role in folklore as well as myth and religion. In many folktales a hero or heroine is given three chances to guess the answer to a riddle before a wish can be granted, or must accomplish three tasks in order to win their reward. In baseball, each batter has three chances to hit a good pitch. The life cycle consists of birth, life and death. In Christianity, God is viewed as a holy trinity: the Father, the Son, and the Holy Ghost. Human beings are seen as consisting of body, mind and soul. The common proverbial expression says: "Third time is a charm." and "All good things come in threes." Time is seen as consisting of past, present and future. The triangle has both positive ("pyramid power") and negative ("love triangle") potentials. The three "kingdoms" of matter are animal, vegetable and mineral.

- "7" is considered a lucky number by most North Americans because in the game of craps, "7" is a winning number on the first throw of the dice. In a much broader sense, however, the number has long been viewed as the symbol of completeness or totality, as seen in the following systems: the Seven Seas (the whole world): In ancient times, this referred to the Mediterranean Sea, the Caspian Sea, the Black Sea, the Red Sea, the Adriatic Sea, the Arabian Sea and the Persian Gulf; in modern times, it refers to the North Atlantic, South Atlantic, North Pacific, South Pacific, Indian, Antarctic, and Arctic Oceans; in astronomy, there are the original 7 planets: Sun, Moon, Mercury, Venus, Mars, Jupiter and Saturn representing the entire solar system; there are 7 days in a whole week, which represents the complete process of the creation of the universe; the 7 colours of the rainbow which is the entire spectrum: red, orange, yellow, green, blue, indigo and violet; the 7 levels of Heaven and 7 levels of Hell; and there are 7 whole notes in the entire musical scale.

- "10" is seen as the Pythagorean symbol of perfection or completeness. It is often used to represent a "perfect score" as in "ten out of ten."

- "13" is considered an unlucky number. Some buildings do not have a 13th floor or room #13; and no one wants to live in a house whose address is 13. Apollo 13 was the only unsuccessful mission by the United States of America's NASA program to land astronauts on the moon. The reason 13 is considered unlucky is because at Jesus Christ's last supper, there were 13 people around the table: Jesus Christ and the 12 apostles, and Judas betrayed Jesus Christ. It was said that there were 13 steps that led to a gallows. Friday, the 13th of any month is considered to be a very unlucky day, because it is said that Jesus Christ was crucified on a Friday.

- "666": The number "6" by itself has no special significance to North American English speakers, but most would recognize "666" as the symbol of "the Antichrist," and a way of invoking him by writing or speaking of "666," as the proverb goes: "Speak of the Devil, and he shall appear." Some people find the 666 sequence to be so inauspicious that they would avoid such a street address, apartment, telephone or license plate number. Many even believe that the common hand signal for "OK" (thumb and index finger touching to form a circle, with the other three fingers lined up straight) is a satanic sign of 666.

In Chinese Culture:

In Chinese culture, numbers seem to play a very important part and they are mostly associated with homonyms. Odd numbers are considered *yáng* or masculine, and even numbers are *yīn* or feminine. Generally speaking, even numbers are preferred more than odd numbers for many events with the exception of 4. For example, people prefer to get married on even number dates rather than odd number dates.

- "1" (yī) indicates the undivided whole, completeness and oneness. There is a saying: "yìxīn yíyì" which means complete devotion to someone or something. "1" is also the number that begets all other numbers. And yet it is considered by some people as not so good a number because it signifies "alone" and "loneliness."

- "2" (èr) is considered a good number because it indicates a pair. Pairing up things and people is lucky, so a wedding is dubbed as double happiness. There is a common saying: "Good things come in pairs, hǎoshì chéng shuāng."

- "3" (sān) is good; it stands for the harmony of heaven, earth and humanity. In Chinese Culture, as Laozi said: "One engendered two; two engendered three; and three engendered everything." The traditional Chinese universe consists of "three powers": heaven, earth, and humanity. There are three co-existing belief systems in traditional China, the Three Teachings: Confucianism, Taoism, and Buddhism. The Three Immortals who represent the three attributes of a good life are: Blessings (fú), Prosperity (lù), and Longevity (shòu).

- "4" (sì) is considered unlucky; its pronunciation sounds too much like "death" (sǐ). Some Chinese avoid this number like the plague, so some buildings or department stores may not have a fourth floor, and some hotels or apartment buildings may not have a room number 4. However, 4 has not always been an unlucky number because traditionally there are: Four Blessings: good fortune, a high salary, longevity and happiness; 4 divine creatures: vermillion bird, white tiger, azure dragon and black tortoise; 4 plants of virtue: the plum, orchid, bamboo and chrysanthemum and 4 kinds of happiness: rain after a long drought, chancing upon an old friend somewhere, the wedding night, and passing an important examination.

- "5" (wǔ) is not good for some people, because it sounds like "wú" (to have not or have nothing), so it is a number to be avoided in business. Again, traditionally there are several things associated with "5" but they are not necessarily all bad. These are the 5 elements: water, fire, earth, wood and metal; the 5 grains: corn, millet, wheat, soybean and rice; the Five Blessings: longevity, wealth, health, virtue, and a natural death; and the 5 poisonous animals: the snake, scorpion, centipede, toad and spider.

- "6" (liù) is good; its alternative pronunciation is "lù" and that sounds like the word for "official salary, lù." "6" is associated with the 6 relationships: these are traditionally defined as father and son, older brother and younger brother, husband and wife; or in modern times, father, mother, older brother, younger brother, wife and child; the 6 domesticated animals: cows, horses, sheep, pigs, chickens and dogs; the 6 mediums of sensing as in the Buddhist saying: "all six mediums of sensing are clean, liùgēn qīngjìng": eye, ear, nose, tongue, body and mind; and the 6 master organs as in the Daoist saying: "the six spirits have taken leave of their master organs, liùshén wúzhǔ": heart, lungs, liver, kidneys, pancreas and gall bladder.

- "7" (qī) is not considered good for some people because it sounds like "qì, abandon, abandoned or giving up." But again, there are many non-negative "7": there are the 7 fairy sisters, the 7 sages of the bamboo grove, the Confucian 7 emotions — happiness, anger, sadness, fear, love, hate and desire; and the folk saying of "7 things we need soon from the outset, kàimén qījiàn shì": firewood, rice, oil, salt, sauce, vinegar and tea.

- "8" (bā) is an excellent number because it sounds rather like "prosper, fā" so it is linked with wealth and prosperity and is the most sought-after number today. It is said that "8" is also linked with Buddhism because the lotus flower has 8 petals. Traditionally we see the 8 immortals, each of whom possesses a special power; each person has his/her "8 characters, bāzì" denoting birth time, day, month and year, each of which is represented by 2 Chinese characters. In modern times, people favor street or house numbers that contain "8." People pay a very high price for license plates or cell phone numbers that contain some "8"s or better yet, all "8"s. "8" rose to national preference when the Summer Olympics opening ceremony was held in Beijing at 8 minutes and 8 seconds after 8 p.m. on August 8, 2008, thus forming a series of "8"s: 8:08:08, 8/8, 2008.

- "9" (jiǔ) is considered to be a good, lucky number. It is the most potent of all single digit numbers because it is the highest *yáng* number. It is often used to mean a high or large number. It also sounds like "long time, long lasting, jiǔ" so it represents eternity and longevity. Historically, "9" is closely associated with the emperor whose robe is embroidered with 9 dragons. There is a nine-dragon wall, which represents the emperor, in the Beihai Park in Beijing. It is said that the Forbidden City has 9999 and a half rooms. "9" is also an important number for businesses who often use it in some way. Some banks and restaurants have a fish tank with 9 gold fish in it for good luck. In Chinese myth, there were 10 suns which threatened human life, so the hero Yi shot down 9 suns and saved humanity from a solar holocaust. The underworld is known as "9 springs, jiǔquán."

- "10" (shí) signifies perfection, completeness or totality. There are many expressions in Chinese that contain "shí," for example: "full, complete, shífēn," "totally satisfied, shízú," "complete, shíquán" and "perfect, perfection, shíquánshíměi."

- Numbers 1 to 10, and hundred, thousand and ten thousand are cleverly used in a sequence to express auspicious things for a Chinese New Year's wish: One [whole] sailing with favorable winds; Two dragons soaring in the sky; Three "Yang" windfalls; Four seasons mild as spring; Five blessings come to your door; Six times six conveniences; Seven stars shining on you; Eight directions bringing you wealth; Nine times nine all safe and sound; Ten out of ten perfect scores; Hundreds of events going smoothly; Thousands of events all auspicious; Myriad events all as you wish.

Animals and Birds

In North American Culture:

- **Ass:** Another name for "donkey," an ass or a jackass is a foolish, irritating, or contemptible person.

- **Beaver:** This industrious builder of dams symbolizes a very busy and hardworking person, as in "busy as a beaver." It is an emblem of Canada.

- **Dove:** This gentle bird traditionally symbolized spirituality and the soul, but in more recent times it has taken on political connotations, standing for peace, pacifists and pacifism, most often in contrast to the hawk, a political symbol of pro-militarism.

- **Eagle:** Often pictured clutching arrows (symbol of war) in its left claws and an olive branch (symbol of peace) with its right claws, this emblem of the United States stands alludes to the desire for peace but the willingness to fight to preserve it.

- **Fox:** As in many cultures, North Americans see the fox as clever, crafty or cunning. The words "fox" or "foxy" have become slang in North American English for an individual, usually a female, with sex appeal. The word "vixen," meaning a female fox, is also used to describe an attractive woman although it tends to imply that the woman in question is being intentionally seductive. There seems to be no North American equivalent to the famous "fox spirit" of Chinese folklore.

- **Hawk:** In ancient Egypt it symbolized the soul, but in modern North America it has political connotations, standing for pro-militarism. This may be because the hawk is a carnivore which attacks and feeds on smaller animals.

- **Lion:** This "king of all beasts" symbolizes power and ferocity, often referred to in contrast to its opposite, the timid and innocent lamb.

- **Mule:** The mule, which is supposed to be "a beast of burden," is also known for having a mind of its own, and not being amenable to persuasion. Therefore, it has become a metaphor for someone who is stubborn or obstinate.

- Owl: Owls are associated with wisdom, possibly because they have great ability to predict weather and they are able to see clearly at night. Since they are nocturnal hunters, they are also associated with death. At the same time, some people put a wooden owl on their roof to ward off birds, rodents and other undesirable elements.

- Phoenix: This mythological bird is associated with the sun, and like the sun that rises anew each day, the phoenix obtains new life by arising from the ashes of its predecessor.

Fig. 6 Phoenix Rising from the Ashes
by Yvonne Walls

- Rat: Since the rat has always been associated with evil-doing, it has become a metaphor for a despicable, deceitful, disloyal person.

- Stork: The stork is associated with fertility and fidelity. Some people believe they bring good luck so they are allowed to build their nest on chimneys where they may bring up their young. In popular culture, they are believed to deliver babies to mothers in a bundle which they hold in their beak.

- Vulture: Since this bird feeds upon the corpses of dead animals, it may be used as a metaphor for a contemptible person who preys upon or exploits vulnerable people. Colloquially, a "culture vulture" is a person with an extreme interest in cultural matters and events.

In Chinese Culture:

- Bat: In European traditions, the bat is a symbol associated with harm and evil, but in China it is a symbol of blessing and fortune, because its name is pronounced "fú," which is also the pronunciation of "good fortune." Often five bats are depicted together, representing "the Five Blessings": long life, prosperity, good health, virtue, and a natural death. The image of a red bat is particularly auspicious, because the pronunciation of "red, hóng" is the same as that of the character for "enormous", so a red bat would symbolize "enormous good fortune."

- Crane: One of many different symbols of longevity, often shown together with a pine tree and a stone (two more longevity symbols), or with a tortoise.

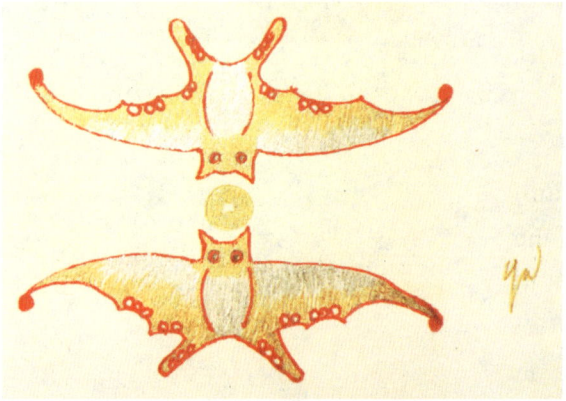

Fig. 7   Bats   by Yvonne Walls   Fig. 8   Crane   by Yvonne Walls

- Deer: Since the pronunciation of "deer, lù" is homophonous with the character for "official salary," it is symbolic of wealth and good fortune.

- Dove: Symbolic of fidelity and longevity, perhaps because doves mate for life, and both sexes are involved in raising their young. It also symbolizes peace in modern times.

CROSS-CULTURAL PERSPECTIVES: NORTH AMERICA AND CHINA

- Dragon (lóng): Unlike a Western dragon, the Chinese dragon is long and slim, has no wings, and does not spit fire. It is also a benevolent creature associated with water which can relieve draughts and extinguish fires. It is a symbol of masculine power, and if it has five toes it symbolizes the Emperor. The dragon pictured together with a phoenix symbolizes Emperor and Empress. Nowadays dragon has become a symbol of China and the Chinese.

Fig. 9   Dragon   by Yvonne Walls

- Fish: A symbol of wealth and abundance. The pronunciation of the Chinese word for fish is identical to that of the word for "abundance," so "to have fish, yǒu yú" sounds like "to have abundance, yǒu yú."

Fig. 10   Fish   by Yvonne Walls

- Fox: Symbolic of cunning, as in the West, but with some additional powers in Chinese folktales: as the fox ages, it acquires the supernatural ability to transform itself into an attractive human female who may attempt to seduce a naive student.

- Phoenix (fènghuáng): In ancient times, it was believed that the appearance of this mythological bird was a sign that the land is being ruled by a just sovereign. Pictured together with a dragon, they become a symbol of the Emperor and Empress, or simply a husband and wife. And when they are together, they also "present auspiciousness."

Fig. 11   Phoenix   by Yvonne Walls

- Qilin: This mythological animal, qílín, sometimes translated as "Chinese unicorn" because it is sometimes depicted with one horn, is described as having the body of a deer, the tail of an ox, the scales of a fish, and cloven hoofs. It is a symbol of peace, good fortune and longevity. It is also an auspicious symbol of a large family with many children. The saying goes: "Qilin brings children (sons)," much like the Western folk belief that the stork brings children.

Fig. 12   Qilin   by Yvonne Walls

- Tiger: In China, the tiger is seen as the king of all beasts, and is a symbol of power, courage and bravery. It is believed to have the power to ward off demonic forces, and therefore stone tiger statues may be seen guarding graves.

- Tortoise: Because of its long lifespan, the tortoise has always been a symbol of longevity in China. Also, due to the round shape of its upper shell (like the vault of heaven above) and the flatness of its lower plate (like the earth, which was believed to be flat), it has been seen as a replica of the cosmos, and was believed to contain the secrets of the universe.

- Yuanyang: Yuānyāng is often translated as Mandarin ducks or love ducks. They are believed to be lifelong couples, so they are symbols of love and fidelity. They often appear as a symbol of conjugal love in art and literature.

Fig. 13   Yuanyang   by Yvonne Walls

- Zodiacal Animals: In traditional Chinese culture, time has been measured in 12-year cycles, and each of the 12 years is symbolized by a different animal, always in this order: Rat, Ox, Tiger, Rabbit, Dragon, Snake, Horse, Goat, Monkey, Rooster, Dog, Pig. Each animal in the zodiac has its own characteristic personality, which is seen as influencing the compatibility of people born in different years.

Flowers and Plants

In North American Culture:

- Carnation: The pink carnation symbolizes gratitude, while the white carnation symbolizes remembrance. On Mother's Day (second Sunday in May), it is customary for children to present carnations to their mothers. Some people wear a red carnation if their mother is alive, and a white carnation if their mother has passed away. Yellow carnations are seen as cheerful.

- Daisy: In North America, the white daisy is a symbol of innocence, simplicity, purity and patience. They are seen as bringing sunshine into people's lives.

- Forget-me-not: This flower is a symbol of true love and remembrance. It is a symbolic reminder for the recipient to remember the person who gives the flowers.

- Poppy: This flower symbolizes resurrection and immortality as the poppy never really dies but just renews and ascends. The red of the poppy could symbolize the blood in sacrifice. For this reason, around Remembrance day (November 11) in Canada and Memorial Day (May 31) and Veterans Day (November 11) in the U.S., poppies are worn by veterans and those who honor the soldiers who sacrificed their lives.

Fig. 14   Rue   by Yvonne Walls

- Rue: The perennial evergreen shrub symbolizes virtue because it is believed that it drives away evil. The rue is also a symbol of sorrow.

- Rose: The symbol of love and romance, especially the red rose. Roses are given to loved ones each year on Valentine's Day and on other special occasions. The white rose represents purity and holiness, the red rose means passion while the yellow rose means wisdom and joy. The rose is the floral emblem of the United States.

In Chinese Culture:

- Bamboo: A symbol of endurance, strength, uprightness and flexibility because it is green in all seasons, bends easily but quickly returns to its original upright position. It is often used as a symbol for an upright person who cannot be corrupted.

- Chrysanthemum: Blooming in autumn, the chrysanthemum symbolizes longevity and the ability to endure harsh circumstances.

- Lotus: Blossoming in the summer, the lotus grows out of the mud and mire, but emerges unstained, so it is a symbol of purity and enlightenment, even though surrounded by impurity.

Fig. 15   Orchid   by Yvonne Walls

- Orchid: The orchid is considered to be one of the "four nobles," together with the plum blossom, chrysanthemum and bamboo. It has always been cherished by virtuous people because orchids evoke the qualities of humility, integrity and refinement, especially as they represent those who are out of favour in government, living solitary lives. It is known as the true noble one.

- Peony: Known as the Queen of Flowers, the peony represents wealth and distinction.

- Pine tree: One of the "Three Friends in Winter" (pine, bamboo and plum tree), the

Fig. 16   Peony   by Yvonne Walls

Fig. 17   Plum Blossom   by Yvonne Walls

pine tree is a symbol of endurance, longevity and fidelity, because it remains green all year round and lives for a long time.

- Plum Blossom: An auspicious symbol of beauty and gentleness because it is a lovely and delicate flower whose blooming in late winter signifies the coming of spring.

Non-verbal Behaviour and Body Language

Non-verbal Behaviour

In any act of communication, the non-verbal cues (the behavioral context) always carry more weight than the words themselves (the verbalized content). English, French and Spanish speaking North Americans may differ greatly in their non-verbal communication norms. English and Chinese non-verbal communication norms and expectations often differ even more greatly, and if not understood may result in miscommunication.

Proxemics

The average physical distance between two speakers of the same language is usually established and maintained without even thinking about what is normal. We all have unconscious expectations about the distance we should establish and maintain for public speaking, social interaction, personal communication, and intimate relations.

Generally in North America, no matter whether people are waiting for a bus, lining up to buy tickets or lining up to pay a cashier, the distance between people will be greater than most Chinese would expect. In China, under similar circumstances, the distance between people will be much closer and seem more crowded. When a Canadian or American stands in line in China, leaving a "normal" space behind the person ahead, a local Chinese may come and stand in the space, because a Chinese may not know this person is actually waiting in line. On the other hand, if a Chinese stands in line, a Canadian or an American may feel this person is rather rude, because the person is so close and has invaded the other's personal space.

E. T. Hall (1966) in his book *The Hidden Dimension* has calculated the average distances maintained by English speaking North Americans in different relationships as follows:

• Intimate: 18 inches (46 cm)

• Personal: 18 inches — 4 feet (46 cm — 1.2 m)

• Social: 4 — 12 feet (1.2 m — 3.6 m)

• Public: 12 — 25 feet (3.6 m — 7.6 m)

Fig. 18   Distance Farther Apart When Not Knowing Each Other Well   by Yvonne Walls   Fig. 19   Distance Closer When More Intimate   by Yvonne Walls

Since Chinese traditionally are more group oriented and the idea of an individual's personal space has not been very strong, the average distance maintained between Chinese speakers is usually shorter than that of North Americans, except between members of opposite sex. Chinese appear to be more tolerant of closer proximity. Chinese might feel less uncomfortable in crowded buses or trains than their average North American counterpart.

Eye Contact

For North Americans, eye contact is very important because it is regarded as a sign of honesty and sincerity. It means: "I have nothing to hide." On the other hand, staring at someone, even at a stranger, is regarded as impolite. Avoiding any eye contact with a person one is talking to shows boredom, disinterest, displeasure or perhaps shame or even guilt. Winking at someone may indicate flirtation, friendliness or amusement, or it may be a signal that one is just "kidding" about what has just been said.

Fig. 20 Good Eye Contact and Firm Handshake   Fig. 21   Gaze Avoidance   by Yvonne Walls
by Yvonne Walls

Eye contact for Chinese speakers also shows honesty and sincerity, but one also has to be careful of sustained eye contact. Occasional gaze aversion is particularly necessary if the interaction or conversation is between a male and a female. In this case, the avoidance of eye contact shows modesty or non-aggressive intent. Usually a superior can look at a subordinate, or an older person at a younger person with sustained gaze without being considered impolite. Winking is not a polite gesture and is rarely practiced.

Interpersonal Synchronization

When taking part in a meeting, the person who chairs the meeting usually speaks first in a North American situation. The people in the meeting may take turns to speak by "going around the table," or whoever feels they have something to contribute may simply speak up. During normal conversation, there is no particular order to observe. Whoever has something to say can speak. It is not considered polite to dominate a conversation, but whoever has something to contribute to the conversation can just jump right in by saying: "Excuse me." In case two people start to talk at the same time, they would say: "Excuse me!" or "Sorry!" and one of them will invite the other speak first. When walking or going in or out of a door, it is usually "ladies first," regardless of seniority. When walking together with several people, one should try to fit into the pattern.

In a Chinese situation, during a meeting, the person who chairs speaks first and then there often will be a speaking order that everyone is expected to follow. During a normal conversation, generally people will yield to the senior in rank or age to speak first and everyone else listens. Interruption is considered impolite even when the intention is to support what the speaker is saying. When walking or going in or out of a door, usually people will yield to the person senior in rank or age to go first, whether that person is male or female.

Touch

The handshake is very common in the West. Newly introduced people shake hands, as do friends who have not seen each other for a while. A good handshake is expected to be firm to show sincerity. To be polite, a man generally waits for a woman to extend her hand before offering to shake hands. Hugging is also common among good friends when they meet and when they say goodbye. Kissing on the mouth, or more commonly on the cheek, between sexes may happen in public places more than one would expect to see in China. However, in this respect, Canadians are somewhat more conservative than Americans.

When introduced, Chinese generally just greet each other. Because of increased Western contact, handshaking is also often used nowadays. However, the grasp may not be as firm as a Westerner might expect, particularly if the handshaking is between different sexes. This is not because they are not sincere. It is because touching does not come naturally between new acquaintances, and touching between different sexes who do not know each other well may be somewhat embarrassing. On the other hand, Chinese people of the same sex may frequently be seen holding hands or walking arm in arm to show friendliness, particularly among young people and older people.

Silence

In a North American situation, although traditionally the advice "silence is golden" is given to children, most people will feel awkward if there are long periods of silence during meetings or conversation. If there is silence, a gap, during a conversation, someone will think of something to say just to "fill the gap." This is partly because eloquence is viewed as a virtue, and partly because silence could mean "we have nothing to say to each other." During large gatherings when a speaker is talking or a musical performance is in progress, people automatically keep silent out of respect for the speaker or the performers and the other people there.

Most Chinese can tolerate silence during meetings or conversations for a longer duration than North Americans. When there is period of silence, a gap, during a conversation, people do not necessarily rush to break the silence. It is a time to think about what has been said or to reflect on its significance. No one feels embarrassed during a period of silence when no one is talking. Some Chinese may use silence where a North American would say "no." Since a direct "no" or disagreement may be viewed as a confrontation, many people will choose simply not to respond. In this case, silence may mean "no" or "no opinion" or even "I do not agree." Having said this, most Chinese are very sociable people. Sometimes people even chat during large gatherings when a speaker is trying to give a speech, or talk to each other even when a performance is in progress, especially if the occasion is a celebratory one.

Gestures and Body Language

Gestures are a very important component of communication, and they are part of body language. Gestures are culture-specific and many identical gestures may have very different meanings in different cultures, so it is important to understand their meanings in different language-culture environments. Some gestures that are important in one culture may not appear at all in another, so they are not always understandable across cultures.

In North American Culture:

- Agreement: Nodding the head up and down shows agreement, acceptance or acknowledgment.

- Air kiss: This is a fairly intimate social gesture where the lips are pursed as if to kiss, but the lips do not touch the other person. However, sometimes the cheeks may even touch and this kind of symbolic kiss may be accompanied by a sound that imitates a kiss: "mwah." Another variant, used when the two people are not standing face-to-face but are looking at each other from a greater distance is to "blow a kiss." This is done by first kissing the inside of your open hand, fingers straight and close together, then pursing the lips and blowing on the kissed part of the open hand while pointing it in the direction of the other person.

- Anger or hostility: Showing a clenched fist. Sometimes people shake their clenched fist while glaring at the person or people to whom they want to express anger or hostility. A gesture of defiance is shown by positioning both fists at the waist while glaring at the adversary.

- Approval: To show approval, appreciation or agreement, one may extend the thumb upwards with the other fingers closed. This gesture is also used to show someone that a job is well done, and is also known as "thumbs-up." Another way to show approval is to nod the head several times.

- Disapproval: This is the opposite of thumbs-up: thumbs-down. It is done simply by turning the thumbs-up gesture upside down.

- Beckoning: Raise the hand, fingers straight and palm facing up, and bend the wrist and fingers toward your own face or chest several times. A less formal and perhaps even less polite way of beckoning a person to "come here" is to raise the index finger with the back of your hand facing the other party, and repeatedly curl it towards yourself.

- Bored: Yawning with one hand covering the mouth is a way of signaling that "I'm bored," or "I am getting sleepy" or "it's getting late." Sometimes boredom is shown by twiddling both thumbs repeatedly.

- Embarrassed: This gesture is made by covering your face with open palm or palms. It shows that you are embarrassed, disappointed, frustrated, surprised or shocked.

- Greeting: The most common greeting method is the handshake. When performing the handshake, the grasp should be firm to show sincerity. Many Chinese, however, might feel that a very firm handshake is either too intimate, or a sign of intention to dominate. A more casual greeting can be given by just nodding the head.

- Hoping for good luck: This gesture is also known or expressed as "keeping our fingers crossed," which means "let's hope everything goes well," or "let's hope for good luck." This is done by crossing the middle finger over the index finger, with the thumb and other fingers folded. Sometimes people make this gesture behind their back while telling a "little white lie" or while making a promise that they have no intention of keeping.

- "I, me": Indicated by pointing to one's own chest with the index finger or the thumb.

- Impatient: Drumming or tapping fingers tips in succession can indicate impatience or frustration, for example, when a person wants to interrupt a conversation but does not get a chance to do so. It can also be a sign that one has stayed long enough and wants to leave. This action can also mean that a person is thinking about an issue but cannot find a solution yet.

- Insulting someone (very vulgar): This insulting gesture is shown with the middle finger thrust upward, the other fingers closed, and showing the back of the fist. It is sometimes accompanied with a forearm jerk. It is known as "giving someone the finger." It signals intentional insult, contempt or disrespect. It is a very vulgar gesture, for which one should not expect to be forgiven. This is why North Americans often have to stifle a laugh when they see a Chinese speaker pointing at something with their middle finger.

- Kidding: To show that one is just kidding, joking or not being serious, one may wink at the person one is addressing. This action can be misunderstood by Chinese as flirting.

- Money: To indicate money, or that one wants money, one rubs the thumb repeatedly over the tip of the index finger and the middle finger. This action is imitative of counting paper bills.

- "My lips are sealed": To make a sign to tell someone "My lips are sealed" or "Your secret is safe with me," one draws the index finger and thumb across closed lips, as if zipping up the lips.

- No: One may indicate "no" or a disapproving "don't" by shaking an open hand left and right, palm facing the other person, or by turning the head left and right two or three times. Another way is to shake an index finger left and right at someone.

Shaking one's head left and right may also mean "I don't know."

- Nonsense: When one makes a circling motion with the index finger pointing to the side of the head, one is saying: "Nonsense!" or "You are crazy!" This is also known as the "screw loose" sign, often used in jest.

- Ok: When the thumb and the index finger touch to form a circle with the other three fingers extended straight with the inside of the hand facing outward, it means "okay," "fine," "great," "perfect" or "no problem."

- Pointing: When people want to point at someone or something, they point at it with the index finger. For North Americans, this is not seen as an impolite gesture.

- Puzzled: This is shown by scratching one's head when one is puzzled, doubtful, confused or unable to understand something.

- Scorn: Pointing one's thumb at one's own nose while wiggling the extended fingers at someone; sometimes this action is accompanied by the sound: "na-na-na-na naaa, naaa." This action, which is a vulgar way of showing scorn directed at another, is also known as "giving someone the raspberries."

- "Shame on you": When a person wants to convey the meaning of "shame on you," he rubs one index finger over the top of the other index finger two or three times. This is to show others that they have done something inappropriate or shameful.

- Shush: To stop a person or other people from talking or being noisy, one only needs to put an extended index finger pointing upward in front of lips to call for silence. Sometimes, this gesture is accompanied by the sound "sh... ."

- Smile: The smile shows friendliness. One can smile at acquaintances or at strangers, just to show a friendly attitude toward them. Sometimes a smile may show agreement or assent.

- Solidarity: Expressed by raising a clenched fist above the head, palm side facing the front, often accompanied by the shouting of slogans.

- Stop: Holding one's arm straight out with the palm facing the addressee is a way of telling that person to stop or stand still.

- Surprise: Raising the eyebrows shows that a person is surprised.

- Uncertainty: This is shown by lifting both shoulders up, sometimes with both hands open, palms facing upward. It is a way of showing uncertainty, not knowing how to answer a question, or sometimes not caring about the answer.

- Victory sign: Raise the index and middle fingers to form a "V," with the palm facing outward. For some people, the inward/outward distinction is very important, because if the palm is facing inward, it becomes a very insulting sign. On the other hand, sometimes people do not notice whether the palm is facing outward or inward.

- Waving "hello" or "goodbye": Extend the arm outward and upward with the palm open, moving the entire hand left and right, facing outward. This gesture can also be used to attract attention. A more informal way of saying goodbye is just to nod one's head.

- Yes: To show one agrees or to say "yes," one nods the head up and down.

In Chinese Culture:

Chinese generally do not use very many gestures. They often think that North Americans communicate more with their hands and their many facial expressions, while Chinese talk with their mouths without much expression on their faces. When a Chinese does use gestures to accentuate what he is talking about, people will describe him as "hands waving and feet dancing, shǒuwǔ zúdǎo" or "gesturing with hands and drawing with feet, bǐshǒu huàjiǎo." Chinese do not shrug shoulders or make the "okay" sign, since the English letter "o" could be taken to mean the Arabic numeral "0." The extended middle finger is not necessarily offensive for them. Actually one may see Chinese people pointing or indicating the number "1" with the middle finger, instead of the index finger.

- Approval: "Thumbs-up" is a positive gesture often used by Chinese now. It means approval, great, marvelous, wonderful and excellent.

- Beckoning: Arm extended, palm facing downward, wave the fingers toward the person, like a scratching action. The gesture for asking a young child or a pet dog to come over is to extend the index finger and bend it towards oneself several times.

- Bothered by something: When something is bothering a person or when he feels that something is not going right, he raises his right hand and starts to scratch his head. This action may also mean one does not know what to do.

- Counting: When Chinese count from 1 to 10 with their hands:

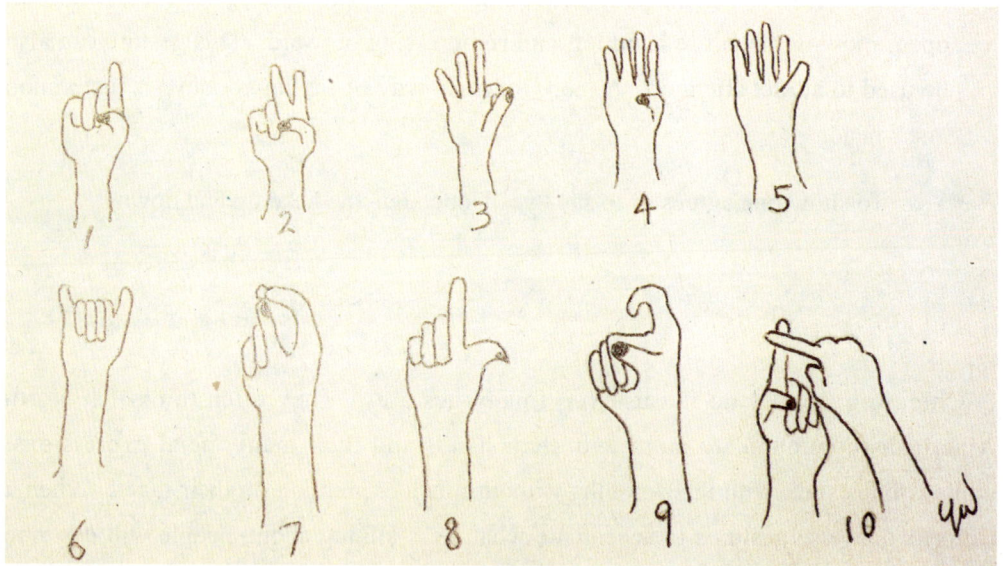

Fig. 22 Counting from 1 to 10 by Yvonne Walls

- Direction: When one is busy or somewhat occupied, one indcates the direction of left, right or front by pointing with one's chin towards that direction. A thumbs-down sign is often used to indicate "under there" or "below."

- Eat: When Chinese want to indicate it is time to eat or to invite someone to eat, they make a gesture of holding a bowl with their left hand and start to move their right index finger and middle finger towards the mouth, as if eating from the bowl using chopsticks.

- Handshake: The handshake is rather common among Chinese now. When a Chinese man shakes hands with another man, he may do it several times to show his sincerity. However, when he shakes hands with a woman, he will just touch her hand or her fingers quickly. This is done so as not to display too much physical contact or to show unnecessary intimacy.

- "I, me": Pointing to one's own nose with the index finger.

- No: Shaking the head left and right.

- Scorn or disdain: To show scorn or disdain for something, a Chinese may make a fist and then extend the little finger outward and upward. This is also used to show something is the least of its kind or unworthy of consideration.

- Shame, shame!: Rub the cheek with the tip of the index finger repeatedly in a downward direction ("face" being symbolic of dignity, "losing face" brings shame).

- Show shame: Chinese often bow down their heads when being scolded, or feel shame or feel they have lost face.

- Shush: To stop a person or other people from talking or being noisy, one only needs to put the extended index finger pointing upward in front of, but not touching, one's lips to call for silence.

- Smile: Smiling shows friendliness, understanding or agreement. However, Chinese generally do not smile at strangers. Smiles can also mean encouragement or comforting. One may notice a Chinese slightly smile when he is told something sad. This is done when one does not know what to say, and can only give a comforting smile. Many Chinese will give a smile when they are unsure how to react or how to respond to a situation.

- Surprise: When one is surprised or taken aback, the first reaction is to open the mouth wide without saying anything.

- Thanks: To show thanks, Chinese may nod the head or bow slightly. Sometimes, they may come forward and use both hands to shake the other's hand several times.

- Uncertainty or embarrassment: When Chinese are uncertain about something or when they are embarrassed, they may giggle or give a short laugh, meaning they do not quite know what should be said.

- Victory sign: Raise the index and middle fingers, keeping them apart, palm facing outwards. This sign can mean "2" in the context of numbers, or scissors if the index finger and the middle finger are brought together in a cutting motion a couple of times.

- Waving "hello" or "goodbye": Raise the arm, palm outward, and move the hand from side to side. Another way of saying goodbye is to raise the palm upward, facing outward, and moving the fingers up and down.

- Yes: Nodding the head up and down.

Impolite Behaviour

For North Americans:

- Boasting (unless obviously joking).

- Burping in front of people.

- Coughing while facing people.

- Eating while walking.
- Pointing at people publicly.
- Spitting in public.
- Staring at strangers.
- Talking loudly, particularly in public spaces.
- Yawning openly before people.

For Chinese:

- Paying the bill in front of your guests in a restaurant.
- Pointing at people with the index finger (although some young people may find it acceptable).
- Refilling your own wine glass or teacup without first offering to refill a guest's.
- Resting a foot on a table or sitting on a table while talking.
- Sitting down before being invited by the host.
- Sustained eye contact.
- "Toying around" or pointing with chopsticks while dining.

Proverbial Wisdom

Proverbial expressions are distillations of widely accepted "pearls of wisdom" circulated and handed down from generation to generation. It is interesting and important to find out and to know that there are similar or even identical proverbial expressions in North American culture and Chinese culture because it shows that basically these two cultures have more in common than meets the eye. Even though they may be expressed somewhat differently, these different ways simply serve the same purpose, just as different expressions are used to express the same wisdom. Therefore, as we can also see from the following list of parallel proverbs, there are indeed different ways of expressing the same cultural values, so different paths may lead to the same goal.

　　谚语和成语是智慧的结晶，是一代一代传下来的。这是公认的事实。知道在北美和中国有同样或相似的说法很有意思，也很重要，因为我们从中就知道这两种文化，事实上有很多相同的地方。虽然它们的述说方式多少不一样，但是这些不同的述说方式还是为了达到相同的目标，即不同的说法表达同样的智慧。下列中英文对照的谚语和成语便表现出两方有很多同样或同等的说法和文化结晶，因之，这两种文化可以说是殊途同归的。

English Proverbial Expressions	中文谚语和成语
A baker's wife may bite of a bun, a brewer's wife may bite of a tun.	近水楼台先得月
A bad conscience is a snake in one's heart.	做贼心虚
A bad penny always comes back.	恶有恶报

A bad workman quarrels with his tools.	劣工嫌器
A bird in the hand is worth two in the bush.	多得不如现得
A black plum is as sweet as a white.	白猫黑猫,抓到老鼠就是好猫
Accidents will happen.	天有不测风云
Actions speak louder than words.	坐而言不如起而行
A clear conscience is a soft pillow.	白天不做亏心事,夜半敲门心不惊
A closed mouth catches no flies.	病从口入,祸从口出
A contented mind is perpetual feast.	知足常乐
Adversity makes strange bedfellows.	身处逆境不择友
A fall into the pit, a gain in your wit.	经一事,长一智
A friend in need is a friend indeed.	患难见真情
After meat, mustard.	雨后送伞
A good appetite is the best sauce.	饥不择食
A heavy snow promises a good harvest.	瑞雪兆丰年
A honey tongue, a heart of gall.	口蜜腹剑／笑里藏刀／佛口蛇心
A Jack of all trades and master of none.	万事皆通,一无所长
A little is better than none.	聊胜于无
A little leak will sink a great ship.	千丈之堤,溃于蚁穴
A little learning is a dangerous thing.	浅学误人
A little spark kindles a great fire.	星星之火,可以燎原
All good things came to an end.	天下无不散之宴席
All his geese are swans.	老王卖瓜,自卖自夸
All rivers run into the sea.	百川入海
All roads lead to Rome.	处处有路到长安
A man gets to know his companion on a long journey and in a little inn.	路遥知马力,日久见人心

A miss is as good as a mile.	失之毫厘，差之千里
A Monday morning quarterback.	事后诸葛亮
Among the blind the one-eyed man is king.	山中无老虎，猴子称霸王
An enemy's mouth seldom speaks well.	狗嘴里吐不出象牙来
An uncut gem goes not sparkle.	玉不琢，不成器
A word spoken is an arrow let fly.	一言既出，驷马难追
A stitch in time saves nine.	小洞不补，大洞吃苦
A straw shows which way the wind blows.	一叶知秋
As you make your bed so you must lie on it.	自食其果
As wet as a drowned rat.	湿得像落汤鸡
Bad news travels fast.	好事不出门，坏事传千里
Beauty is in the eye of the beholder. / Beauty lies in lovers' eyes.	情人眼里出西施
Beggars can't be choosers.	饥不择食
Better an open enemy than a false friend.	明枪易躲，暗箭难防
Better a small fish than an empty dish.	有胜于无
Better be the head of an ass than the tail of a horse.	宁为鸡头，不为凤尾
Better the devil you know than the devil you don't.	明枪易躲，暗箭难防
Better to sail slowly than not to sail at all.	不怕慢，就怕站
Birds of a feather flock together.	物以类聚
Bite off more than one can chew.	贪多嚼不烂
Bite the hand that feeds one.	恩将仇报
By others' faults, wise men correct their own.	他山之石，可以攻玉
Cast pearls before swine.	对牛弹琴

Caught between the devil and the deep blue sea.	进退维谷 / 进退两难
Clothes make the man.	人靠衣裳，马靠鞍装
Clothes do not make the man.	人不可以貌相
Comparisons are odious.	人比人，气死人
Constant dripping wears away the stone.	滴水穿石
Courtesy costs nothing.	礼多人不怪
Covet all, lose all.	贪多必失
Cut the coat according to the cloth.	量布裁衣
Deep rivers move in silence, shallow brooks are noisy.	深水静静流，浅溪潺潺流
Despair gives courage to a coward.	人急造反，狗急跳墙
Diamond cut diamond.	强中更有强中手
Diet cures more than the doctor.	药补不如食补
Discretion is the better part of valour.	小心即大勇
Diseases come on horseback, but go away on foot.	病来如山倒，病去如抽丝
Do as you would be done by.	推己及人 / 己所不欲，勿施于人
Don't wash your dirty linen in public.	家丑不可外扬
Don't count your chickens before they are hatched.	勿打如意算盘
Don't cross the bridge until you come to it.	船到桥头自然直
Don't judge a book by its cover.	勿以貌取人 / 人不可貌相
Don't let the grass grow under your feet.	不失时机
Don't put all your eggs in one basket.	不要孤注一掷
Don't put off till tomorrow what should be done today.	今日事，今日毕

Do unto others as you would be done unto.	己所不欲，勿施于人
Drunkenness reveals what soberness conceals.	酒后吐真言
Easier said than done.	说话容易做事难
Easy as pie.	易如反掌
Easy come, easy go.	易得易失
Eat one's cake and have it too.	又要马儿好，又要马儿不吃草
Empty vessels make the most sound.	一瓶子不响，半瓶子晃荡
Even Homer sometimes nods.	人非圣贤，孰能无过 / 智者千虑，必有一失
Even the dog swaggers when its master wins favour.	狗仗人势 / 一人得道，鸡犬升天
Every advantage has its disadvantage.	有利必有弊
Every cook praises his own broth.	王婆卖瓜，自卖自夸
Every dog has his day.	十年河东，十年河西
Every man has his faults.	人孰无过 / 人无完人
Everyone to his taste.	人各有所好
Every potter praises his own pot./Every salesman boasts of his own wares.	王婆卖瓜，自卖自夸
Fair face, foul heart.	人面兽心
Fame has its price.	人怕出名猪怕肥
Familiarity breeds contempt.	近庙欺神
First come first served.	捷足先登
Fish begins to stink at the head.	上梁不正下梁歪
Fishing in the air.	水中捞月
Forgive and forget.	不念旧恶

Fortune favours fools.	傻子有傻福
Fortune is fickle.	天有不测风云，人有旦夕祸福
Gather ye rosebuds while ye may.	有花堪折直须折
Gild the lily.	画蛇添足
Give him an inch and he'll take a yard/mile.	得寸进尺
God's mill grinds slow but sure.	天网恢恢，疏而不漏
Good medicine tastes bitter.	良药苦口，忠言逆耳
Greatest genius often lies concealed.	大智若愚
Habit is second nature.	习惯成自然
Half a loaf is better than none.	聊胜于无
Hardships never come alone.	祸不单行
Haste makes waste.	欲速则不达
He cries wine and sells vinegar.	挂羊头卖狗肉
He has a tiger by the tail.	骑虎难下
He is lifeless that is faultless.	人孰无过
He is rich enough who owes nothing.	无债就是富
He that sups with the devil must have a long spoon.	敬鬼神而远之
He that lies down with dogs must rise up with fleas./He that touches pitch will be defiled.	近墨者黑
He that will thrive must rise at five.	五更起床，百事兴旺
He who does not gain loses.	无所得即有所失
He who has a mind to beat his dog will easily find his stick.	欲加之罪，何患无辞
He who hesitates is lost.	举棋不定，坐失良机

He who risks nothing, gains nothing.	不入虎穴，焉得虎子
He who would catch fish must not mind getting wet.	欲擒龙王，就得下海
His bark is worse than his bite.	嘴硬心软 / 雷大雨小
Hunger finds no fault with the cookery.	饥不择食
If there were no clouds, we should not enjoy the sun.	吃得苦中苦，方知甜中甜
If we cannot get what we like, we have to like what we can get.	随遇而安
If you agree to carry the calf, they'll make you carry the cow.	得寸进尺
If you cannot bite, never show your teeth.	不能打仗，切莫出兵
If you have no hand, you cannot make a fist.	巧妇难为无米之炊
If you run after two hares, you will catch neither.	两头落空
If you sell the cow, you sell her milk too.	蚀了本也输了利 / 赔上夫人又折兵
If you want something done right, do it yourself.	求人不如求自己
Ill gotten, ill spent.	悖入悖出
In for a penny, in for a pound.	一不做，二不休
In the end things will mend.	船到桥头自然直
In wine there is truth.	酒后吐真言
It is a small flock that has not a black sheep.	家家有本难念的经
It is never too late to learn.	活到老，学到老
It is no use crying over spilt milk.	泼水难收
It never rains, but it pours.	祸不单行
Kill the goose that laid the golden egg.	杀鸡取卵

Knowledge is power.	知识就是力量

Learn to walk before you run.	循序渐进
Leopards cannot change their spots.	江山易改，本性难移
Let bygones be bygones.	既往不咎
Let sleeping dogs lie.	别自找麻烦
Let things take their course.	听其自然
Life has its ups and downs.	十年河东，十年河西
Like a cat on a hot tin roof.	热锅上的蚂蚁
Like a duck to water.	如鱼得水
Like attracts like.	物以类聚，人以群分
Like begets like./Like father, like son.	有其父必有其子
Like cures like.	以毒攻毒
Little strokes fell great oaks.	水滴石穿
Little things amuse little minds.	小人志卑
Live and learn.	活到老，学到老
Look before you leap.	三思而后行
Love is blind.	情人眼里出西施
Love me, love my dog.	爱屋及乌

Make haste slowly.	从容赶急
Make hay while the sun shines.	未雨绸缪 / 趁热打铁
Man proposes, God disposes.	谋事在人，成事在天
Many hands make light work.	众擎易举 / 众人拾柴火焰高
Measure another's corn by one's own bushel.	以己度人
Misery loves company.	同病相怜 / 祸不单行
Misfortunes never come alone.	祸不单行

Money makes the world go 'round. /Money talks.	有钱能使鬼推磨
More apparent than real.	虚有其表
More haste, less speed.	欲速则不达
Much care brings grey hair.	忧虑催人老
Necessity is the mother of invention.	穷则变，变则通
Never cackle till your egg is laid.	事竟成，才声张
New brooms sweep clean.	新官上任三把火
Nobody is perfect.	人无完人
No garden without its weeds.	有利必有弊
No man is a hero to his valet.	近庙欺神
No pains, no gains./ No song, no supper./No sweat, no sweet.	不劳则无获
Nothing comes from nothing.	无风不起浪
Nothing ventured, nothing gained.	不入虎穴，焉得虎子
On the horns of a dilemma.	进退维谷 / 进退两难
One good turn deserves another.	善有善报
Out of debt, out of danger.	无债一身轻
Out of sight, out of mind.	眼不见，心不烦
People who live in glass houses should not throw stones.	正人先正己
Practice makes perfect.	熟能生巧
Pride comes before a fall.	骄者必败
Putting the horse before the cart.	本末倒置

Seeing is believing.	百闻不如一见
Six of one, half dozen of the other.	半斤八两
Speak of the devil and he is sure to appear.	说曹操曹操就到
Spectators see more than players.	旁观者清
Spend money like water.	挥金如土
Still water runs deep.	大智若愚 / 深藏不露
Take things as they come.	既来之，则安之
Tall trees catch much wind.	树大招风
Teaching grandmother to suck eggs.	班门弄斧
The bait hides the hook.	笑里藏刀
The calm after a storm.	否极泰来
The coat makes the man.	佛要金装，人要衣装
The pot calls the kettle black.	五十步笑百步
There are two sides to every story.	公说公有理，婆说婆有理
There's no place like home.	金屋银屋比不上自己草屋
The walls have ears.	隔墙有耳
Throw out a sprat to catch a mackerel.	吃小亏占大便宜 / 抛砖引玉
Time and tide wait for no man.	岁月不等人
Time is money.	寸金难买寸光阴
To fish in troubled waters.	浑水摸鱼
Too many cooks spoil the broth.	七手八脚必败事
Two heads are better than one.	三个臭皮匠，顶个诸葛亮
We reap what we sow.	种瓜得瓜，种豆得豆
What can you expect from a pig but a grunt?	狗嘴里吐不出象牙
What goes around comes around.	善有善报，恶有恶报

What's done cannot be undone.	木已成舟
When in Rome, do as the Romans do.	入乡要随俗
When the cat's away, the mice will play.	阎王不在，小鬼作怪
Where there is smoke there is fire.	无风不起浪
Where there is a will, there is a way.	有志者，事竟成
While there is life, there is hope.	留得青山在，不怕没柴烧
Words cut more than swords.	舌剑利于刀剑
You can't run with the hare and hunt with the hounds.	两面讨好
You can't teach an old dog new tricks.	老狗熊学不会新玩意儿
You get what you pay for.	一分钱，一分货
You must lie in the bed you have made.	自作自受
You can't make a silk purse out of a sow's ear.	狗嘴里吐不出象牙

In conclusion, based on the above observations, we know that there are similarities and differences between North American and Chinese cultures. However, these differences are not right or wrong, they are merely examples of "different paths to the same goal."

郑重声明

高等教育出版社依法对本书享有专有出版权。任何未经许可的复制、销售行为均违反《中华人民共和国著作权法》，其行为人将承担相应的民事责任和行政责任；构成犯罪的，将被依法追究刑事责任。为了维护市场秩序，保护读者的合法权益，避免读者误用盗版书造成不良后果，我社将配合行政执法部门和司法机关对违法犯罪的单位和个人进行严厉打击。社会各界人士如发现上述侵权行为，希望及时举报，本社将奖励举报有功人员。

反盗版举报电话　（010）58581897　58582371　58581879
反盗版举报传真　（010）82086060
反盗版举报邮箱　dd@hep.com.cn
通信地址　北京市西城区德外大街4号　高等教育出版社法务部
邮政编码　100120